52 WEEKS

OF

SALES SUCCESS

D0066151

ALSO BY RALPH R. ROBERTS WITH JOHN GALLAGHER

Walk Like a Giant, Sell Like a Madman

52 WEEKS

OF

SALES SUCCESS

**AMERICA'S #1 SALESMAN SHOWS YOU
HOW TO CLOSE EVERY DEAL!**

RALPH R. ROBERTS

with John Gallagher

HarperBusiness

A Division of HarperCollinsPublishers

HarperCollins books may be purchased for educational, business, or sales promotional use. For information please write: Special Markets Department, HarperCollins Publishers, Inc., 10 East 53rd Street, New York, NY 10022.

658.85
ROB
5/99

FIRST EDITION

Designed by Alma Orenstein

Library of Congress Cataloging-in-Publication Data

Roberts, Ralph R., 1958–
    52 weeks of sales success : America's #1 salesman shows you how to close every deal! / Ralph Roberts ; with John Gallagher.
      p. cm.
    Includes index.
    ISBN 0-88730-963-1
    1. Selling. I. Gallagher, John, 1949– . II. Title.
    III. Title: Fifty-two weeks of sales success.
    HF5438.25.R583   1999
    658.85—dc21   98-43026

99 00 01 02 03 ❖/HC 10 9 8 7 6 5 4 3 2 1

This book is for the Boss and Dot, my parents;

And for Tony Ferris, lawyer, mentor, friend;

And for Betty Tomczak, secretary extraordinaire.

CONTENTS

ACKNOWLEDGMENTS

The authors would like to thank some great folks at Harper-Collins: Executive Editor, David Conti; Publisher, Adrian Zackheim; and Publicist, Amy Lambo; our agent, Jeff Herman; and the employees at Ralph R. Roberts Real Estate, Inc., Summit Title, and Destiny Homes for their help in the preparation of this book, especially Joe Hafner and my wife, Kathy, who read and critiqued the entire manuscript.

We would also like to thank the numerous salespeople and other inspirational people who shared their ideas with us. This book would be poorer but for their help. Among those we want to say a special thanks to are the following:

Lance Avery
Ralph Bianchi
Stella Borst
Howard Brinton
Les Brown
John and Roxann Byars
Jack Canfield
Allan Domb
Judge Pat Donofrio
Dianna Duchene
Dave Ebner
Chuck Ferarolis

Art Fettig
John Gagliano
Shari Goldstein
James A. Good
Mark Victor Hanson
Greg Herder
Stephen J. Hopson
John Jacobs
Liz and Leslie Kiwior
Patty Klein
John Kuczeski
Mike Layne
Dennis LeBlanc
Marty Liebman
Pam Lusczakoski
Stanley Mills
Mark and MaryEllen Paczkowski
Wally and Sally Paczkowski
Frank Palazzolo
Larry Perkins
Roger Petri
Monica Reynolds
Dave and Marcella Roberts
Jeff and Kathy Roberts
Cathy Russell
Joe Sirianni
Lindsay Sokol
Mark Stevens
Greg Sugg
Lew Tuller
Bob and Kathy Van Goethem
Joe and Rosalie Vicari
John Vigi

INTRODUCTION

Hi, I'm Ralph R. Roberts

Let me tell you how this book came to be written.

A couple of years ago, about the time I wrote my first book, *Walk Like a Giant, Sell Like a Madman*, my business was really taking off. True, I already had been the most productive Realtor in the United States for a long time by then. Over the previous 10 years my level of sales had zoomed from 300 transactions a year to 600 per year—almost a hundred times what an average Realtor does each twelve months.

Because of my success, I was getting more and more requests to speak at out-of-town conferences and seminars. I accepted many of the speaking engagements, first, because I enjoy doing them, and, second, because I feel a strong obligation to give something back to the sales profession that has done so much for me.

In addition to being out of town a lot, I was adding pieces to my core business at home. Besides just selling real estate, I created my own mortgage company and my own title company. I had a public relations operation that booked me for radio and television interviews and got my columns placed in various publications. I was stretched a little thin, but I was enjoying myself and looking for new challenges all the time.

One day, my office manager, Mark, stopped me. "Ralph!" he scolded me. "You're always going out of town to teach other people how to be great salespeople. Yet you have all these new employees right here in your own company. Why not hold a seminar for us sometime?"

I thought about his words. And, yes, I saw he was correct. Here I was, jetting to resort cities to speak at major sales conventions yet neglecting some of the vital training I owed my employees back home.

Well, whenever I become aware of one of my own weaknesses, I try to correct it immediately. So I created a series of weekly seminars with my staff. We began to meet every Monday at 10:30 A.M. in a conference room at my headquarters in suburban Detroit.

I worked hard to prepare for these sessions. One day I'd talk about goal setting, and another day we'd discuss time-management techniques. A popular topic was how a salesperson can know what his or her time is worth in dollars and cents. I remember that we debated whether a "hard-sell" technique was more effective than a "soft-sell" approach. Our meetings were lively and often ran well over the one hour allotted for them.

Sometimes I invited other top-notch salespeople to address the group. I found these people to be truly inspiring. The questions that came up again and again were the ones that perplex salespeople the world over: How do I stay motivated? How do I handle all the paperwork? How should I promote myself? I saw that many of these superstars had their own techniques for handling the demands of a sales career. Sometimes these were similar to my own, and sometimes they were different.

As my seminars progressed, I came to realize that I had a second book in me. My Monday morning meetings with my staff could, I saw, amount to a full-fledged course in salesmanship. In the course of a year we covered virtually every topic I had put into my first book with a lot more ideas to spare.

So this second book is, in effect, the written version of the year-long series of seminars that I conducted for my staff. Just as I took one important topic per week for them, I've decided to organize this book around a one-idea-a-week-for–52-weeks principle. You can read the book that way—one chapter per week—or you can read it all in one sitting and dip back into it as you need it. Or you can skip around to the topics that seem especially relevant to you. I've tried to make this book as flexible and as useful for you as I could.

Just as I introduced my staff to some of the nation's top salespeople, I'll let you meet some of them in these pages, too. For example, we'll be meeting Stephen Hopson, a remarkable young man who has won every sales award for stockbrokers that Merrill Lynch can give. And John Gagliano, owner of a phenomenally successful chain of auto collision repair shops. And Patty Klein, a super travel agent here in metro Detroit. And Jonathan Dwoskin, who taught me how to transfer basic sales techniques to the world of the Internet. And many, many more.

It's my goal to help all my readers realize that they, too, can be not only good salespeople, but great ones—true superstars. Sometimes people hear me speak and think that I must possess some magic elixir of success, or that I'm unnaturally talented. Neither is true. I started out in sales like many of you—a green 18-year-old kid with no college who had lots of dreams but not a clue how to make them come true. Thanks to some wonderful mentors and a lot of hard work, I've accomplished every one of my early dreams. Now I'm working on a whole set of new dreams—like boosting my production from 600 transactions a year to 1,000. I know I'll get there someday.

If you take one lesson away from this book, it should be this: Your dreams can become reality. Don't be intimidated, don't be discouraged. We all have bad days, but success is just a matter of following the step-by-step path of progress that others have already laid out for you. I truly expect that this book will teach you a lesson a week to help you succeed. And nothing will make me happier than when you come up to me and say, "Thanks, Ralph, your book helped make me a superstar just like you!"

Getting Started

I got started in selling real estate right out of high school. I probably would have been successful more quickly if I had gone to college, but at that time I was eager to get started and make money. I took $900 in graduation gift money and bought my first home. I was just 18. I'd rent out rooms to friends for $30 or $40 a week. If they didn't have the cash to pay me, I'd have them use their Penney's charge card to buy me a TV set. I remember I had a waterbed upstairs, and it was so heavy that the house sagged to one side.

Getting started was the toughest part of my career, no question. I was fired from two sales jobs because the managers said I had no future in sales. I had one of my first homes foreclosed because I got overextended on all my payments. I was working virtually around the clock, not always productively. I know now that I could have worked more efficiently and reached my level of success even sooner. In this chapter I'd like to give a few tips so you can learn from some of my mistakes.

First, if you're a novice salesperson, it may help to realize certain things. Understand that this is the toughest part of your career. You have no past clients to turn to, no referrals from satisfied customers. You feel all alone, and you probably doubt your ability and your future. A lot of talented people get out of sales at this point. Their careers are over before they really begin.

That's a shame. There are ways to get beyond this break-in period. I was a green kid myself once, handing out my business cards to strangers and not really knowing why, but I went on to heights of success I probably couldn't even dream about them. You can, too.

So, first, I always advise novices to tell everyone they know about their job—everybody from grandparents to old friends from high school. Develop a list and mail out something, then give them a quick call. Maybe you're a travel agent or you're selling cars or computers or home furnishings or stocks and bonds—things that everyone needs and everyone buys sooner or later. Family and friends become the first customers for many such salespeople and you build up from there.

But even if you're selling jet airplanes or complex software, let everyone know what you do. Just because you're selling something your friends and family know nothing about or have no direct connection to, doesn't mean they don't know people you want to be linked to.

Also, stay away from negative people. They have no value in your life. With customers you should always be positive. If someone asks how your business is going, say it is unbelievable. You could be just steps away from bankruptcy, but you have to present a positive outlook. This anti-negative attitude extends to your competition. Never badmouth your rivals. Mudslinging will never help you win your customer. It will probably only backfire.

Get as much training as you can early on. As I said, I did it the other way, postponing my formal training for years while I beat my head against the wall. Now I firmly believe that you can learn from others. There are experts out there willing to help you learn. Take advantage of them. It'll be time and money well spent.

Most of all, remember that if you work hard, things will get better. My friend John Vigi is one of the nation's top stockbrokers. He handles all my accounts and has made me lots of money. But when he started out about 15 years ago, he had no clients and no commissions. John remembers cold-calling as many as 300 people in a row without a single sale. It was discouraging!

It reminds me of when I got my first real estate job. There were these two brothers, Noel and Tony Fox. They owned Fox Brothers Real Estate next to my dad's construction office. The Boss built houses, and they would sell them for him. I remember they were sharp dressers; they always had nice cars and nice suits, and they were mentors and got me started in real estate. They taught me something pretty valuable, which was going door to door to meet people. And that's a hard thing to do. Even before I went door to door, they took me to a grocery store, and they said, "You go in there and meet everybody, give everyone your card, and when you're done giving everyone your card, come back to the office and we'll get started on the next project." Well, I went there in the morning, but new people keep coming in all day long, so basically I never got done. When I got to the office later that night, I said how am I supposed to get done meeting everyone when new people keep coming in? And they said, "Well, that's the idea. You have to meet everybody. Everyone has to know what you do so you can help them." It was great advice, even if I didn't see the wisdom of it at the time.

It's important to remember that all this hard work pays off. John Vigi probably hasn't made cold calls in a long time. He doesn't have to. His portfolio of clients keeps him busy enough to be among Merrill Lynch's top 10 or 15 percent of brokers nationwide. For me it's the same. I don't have to work nearly as hard at selling as I once did. I've established my customer base and hired good assistants, and this frees me to not work so many long hours.

I have a couple of young guys working for me today who are good salespeople but they take time off for hockey games and softball and other stuff. And I tell them, "When I was your age I didn't take any time off. I was building a future." Well, maybe I did take some time off, but I did work every day in my younger years. I try to help them see that by working very, very hard when you're starting out, you'll get to a level of success that's easier to maintain. If I never made another call, I could still sell houses for the rest of my life just from the past customers who call me and from referrals I get. I've sold homes for some customers two, three, four or more times. My hard work is paying off today in more leisure time with my family and more money with which to enjoy it.

So the keys to getting started are to let everyone know what you do; stay in touch with your network of friends and family and contacts, which probably includes at least 250 people. That may sound like a lot, but once you start to add up all the people you know, you'll easily get to 250. Stay in touch, mail something out to them frequently, and get to know everything about your product and your market. If you stick with it, things will improve. I guarantee it.

RALPH'S RULE

Novices need to remember that even the most successful producers started out just like them—alone and afraid. But you can overcome this with hard work and savvy marketing.

Your Yearly Review

One Christmas several years ago, my friend Stanley Mills, one of the top real estate salespeople in Tennessee, asked me about my annual plan. "What annual plan?" I asked sheepishly. Stanley told me if I didn't have an annual plan to guide my efforts I was leaving money on the table. Stanley and I spent a few days working on my first annual plan. It proved so successful for me that today I spend probably two full weeks between Thanksgiving and Christmas each year working on my plan for the following year. It runs to more than 150 pages now and covers every aspect of my business.

Doing this sort of annual planning is just one of the tasks you need to accomplish on a yearly basis. If daily and weekly checklists keep you focused on accomplishing tasks, and a monthly checklist provides some medium-term controls on your activities, your yearly checklist must be used for major life reviews. An annual review and plan is the document that will guide and shape your activities for the year ahead. It can be critical to your growth and success.

An annual plan consists of more than just listing the major projects you want to accomplish in the coming 12 months. It ought to include the how and the why, too. To give you an idea what I mean, here are some things that ought to be covered in your yearly review sessions.

Your Yearly Checklist

1. Break down your yearly goals to day-to-day steps. For example, if I want to sell 700 homes next year and buy 150 new investment properties, my plan will include both the costs involved and the profits to be made. You shouldn't just write something like "Sell 250 cars this year," but break it down like this. "Sell 250 cars a year or five per week or one per day. Selling one car requires on average 50 customer contacts, or five per hour in a 10-hour day. My profit will be $500 from each sale." And so forth. In my plan I'll outline how much time to spend on self-promotion and what kinds of activities that will include—how many speeches out of town, how many radio interviews, how many TV spots. I break down my goals into specific time periods. I try to estimate how many assistants I'll need to accomplish these goals, what I'm going to pay them, how I'm going to motivate them. The more detail you can put in your plan, the better road map you've created for yourself.

2. Review your entire portfolio of investments. Decide if you're making progress toward your goals and make adjustments if necessary. This certainly will require a detailed review with your broker and your tax adviser.

3. Review your goals with your spouse and family or with some other trusted friend. Get their feedback on whether you're on track. Make sure these people know what's most important to you. That way, you can enlist their help in accomplishing your goals. If, for example, you want to lose 50 pounds, letting your loved ones know will enable them to encourage you in an exercise program. And showing them your business goals and the expected rewards will help them understand why you need to spend extra time at the office each week.

4. Sit down with your boss and/or employees for a performance review. If you're the boss, encourage feedback from your workers. Building a team means listening to others. Of course, a good company will be giving little feedback sessions all through the year. What I mean here is that at least on a yearly basis you ought to have a solid idea how you stand in the eyes of your employer. Don't wait for trouble to creep up on you.

5. Attend at least one annual convention in your industry or take at least one continuing education course in your field. Education should never stop. Make it part of your annual business plan to enhance your credentials in this way. Again, you ought to be attending shorter seminars all through the year, but at least once annually you should take advantage of a major educational opportunity.

6. Take at least two weeks' vacation and get out of town. No kidding. Your family deserves at least that much of your undivided attention each year. And you probably need the time off, too.

RALPH'S RULE
Most salespeople work day to day or month to month but never do anything like a good, detailed annual plan. The ones who plan can testify to how much more productive it makes them.

Take Care of Your Customers

We want to take care of our customers. We want to do the very best we possibly can. Sometimes that means going the extra mile. This is especially true if something has gone wrong.

Recently one of my buyer agents came to me with a problem. A customer who had bought a house through us was angry because he moved in and found the seller had left a lot of junk behind. Although I didn't see it myself, my buyer agent confirmed that the house was a disaster. Even though we're not responsible for that, it still left a bad taste in the mouth of the buyer. Like it or not, he's going to associate this bad experience with my company, and you know what that means. He won't do business with us again.

So I called and talked to my buyer and I wanted him to know how valuable he was to me. I told him that I was instructing my agents and my mortgage company that the next time this customer was ready to move or refinance his mortgage, I would write him a check for $500 if he did it with us. I told him that I'd do this because I want him to know that his business means a lot to me. Well, the customer went away happy and I'm sure we've kept him as a future client.

You see, a single deal with a customer means nothing more than one commission. But if you can do what's right for him, you can have him as a client for life. We used to celebrate closing a deal; now we celebrate opening a relationship.

Patty Klein, a super travel agent whom we will meet elsewhere in this book, says that whenever an airfare war ensues, she checks all her clients' airline tickets to see if any of their airfares have been reduced. If they went down, she reissues the tickets at the lower fare and gives her clients a voucher for the difference to be used on a future flight. "I also keep a database of client requests," she says, "so if I see a good rate to a particular destination, I call the client to let them know. I also use reputable consolidators for international travel, which saves my clients hundreds of dollars per trip."

The best sales operations empower their customer contact people to do whatever it takes to satisfy unhappy customers. In my office, we have a rule that any of our people can write a check for up to $100 to take care of any minor problem encountered in one of our deals. Larger than that, I or someone else gets involved, but all the little stuff is to be dealt with immediately.

Greg Sugg, a top GMAC Mortgage official, tells me the best car companies empower their customer service reps to take any immediate action, up to and including taking back a car that's a "lemon." That may seem like a drastic step for a company to take, but in the long run it builds everlasting customer loyalty. Only by doing right by your customers can you expect to keep them for the future.

RALPH'S RULE

A lot of times you'll have to choose between a quick commission or a long-term relationship with a customer. The second-rate salespeople choose the first. The champions choose the second, knowing it's best for both the customer and the salesperson.

Learn from Your Mistakes

I got started in real estate in 1975, right out of high school. I took my graduation money and bought a house in my hometown. It cost $9,000 and I put $900 down and moved in. I did it without bothering to pay for title insurance, which of course ought to have been an essential part of this or any real estate transaction. But I was young and cocky and believed I could do everything myself.

Well, about a year later I found out about what a mistake this was. I had gone to the Indianapolis 500 car race with my friends, and when I got back into town I found that some people had moved into my house. Literally moved right in. I remember they had a couple of dogs and lots of stuff and a rather bogus claim to the property. But my attorney told me that because I had neglected the title search I had two options: I could either move in with them or fight them in court.

As unpleasant as this situation became, I have to say that failing to get a title search turned out to have been one of my more fortunate mistakes. It taught me so much about not cutting corners that thousands of customers and investors who do business with me have benefited from it. I had tried to save a few bucks by skipping the basics. I don't make those kinds of mistakes anymore.

Anyway, the reason people were living in my home was that I had bought it from a woman and her daughter who had no right to sell it to me. Another daughter actually owned the house and let her mom live there, and it was the mom and another daughter who decided to sell it. Well, it cost me $20,000 in legal fees and eight years in court but I finally won my lawsuit. The family had to pay me $6,000 to help me recover some of my legal fees, which of course didn't come close to making up for the money and energy I lost on this deal.

I had thought when I first bought the place that I was a pretty smart guy—right out of school I already had my real estate license, and I thought, "What do I need others for when I can do all the paperwork myself?" A basic title search, which today may cost a homeowner a couple hundred dollars, would have saved me years of aggravation.

Another mistake I made during this whole episode was not settling that case in the beginning. I've been in a number of legal disputes during my 23 years in real estate because, unfortunately, if you deal with thousands of properties over the years, a few bad things are going to arise. But I have never lost a single case, not even one. I've settled some, but never lost. And, as I said, I probably should have settled that first one, too. Because one of the lessons I've learned from my mistakes is that being in court is the last thing you want to do.

This lesson is so basic and it cost me so much time and trouble that I'll say it again. You should always try to work something out. Reaching common ground between parties is always better—better for a husband and wife, better for a landlord and tenant, better for anyone in any sort of dispute. Don't be like the younger Ralph Roberts who thought he could take someone to court just to have his way. As I said, I got my way, but I just didn't realize how much it would cost me to get it.

If I started to list all the mistakes I've made in my real estate career, this book might be about a thousand pages long. I've made every mistake in the book. I've even written an educational brochure that I sell to other Realtors that outlines my 10 top mistakes. It's something I offer to salespeople to help them avoid some of the most common pitfalls.

Among those mistakes: Neglecting my family and killing myself to make a living by working 100-hour weeks. Not having a business plan to guide my efforts. Not getting enough education early on to help me understand the ways of business. Not being smart enough to get the most out of the technology I was collecting all the time. Not paying attention to the needs and goals of my assistants.

Yes, I've made these and many other mistakes, and they've all cost me dearly.

But if there's one mistake that underlies all these other ones, it was thinking I knew all there was to know about a subject. Thinking that I didn't need the advice of others. Thinking that my current way of doing something was the right way. "After all," I would reason, "I'm already a success, right? I sell more homes than any other Realtor in America, right? I'm at the top in my marketplace, so what do I need to learn new ways of doing business for?"

Well, I'm proof that you can always learn from others and always learn better ways of doing things. Almost every day one of the people who works for me comes up with a helpful suggestion. Many, many times an idea that I first laughed at turned out to be something that did me a world of good, once I let myself understand it.

I used to thumb my nose at education courses for salespeople, thinking that I already knew it all. I used to avoid our conventions, not understanding all the great networking and seminars available at these meetings. I never drew up a business plan until about six years ago, thinking I didn't need one because I was already doing 300 transactions a year. Then my friend Stanley Mills helped me draw up my first business plan, which I've followed faithfully. And you know what? My production has doubled to 600 transactions a year.

I'm living proof that the greatest mistake of all is arrogance—an inner conviction that you already know just about anything worth knowing. Maybe I'll never be humble—it would be hard to be in my business and not have a pretty healthy ego. But at least now I'm smart enough to listen to others, to profit by listening to them, and to realize that no matter how smart or successful I get, I'll always have a lot to learn.

RALPH'S RULE
Mistakes can be costly but they can have an upside, too, provided you're willing to change and not make the same mistakes over and over.

From Bartender
to Marketer

I wasn't always the top-producing salesperson I am today. I've had lots of failures in my career. I've fallen on my face. But through it all, I've always been able to roll over and see the sky. And to paraphrase my friend Les Brown, the motivational speaker, I always knew that if I could see up, I could get up.

I think that even in failure I never lost the most important ingredient for sales success—a burning desire to be the best. And, perhaps just as important, I've always been able to learn from my mistakes.

Let me tell you a story about one of my early ventures. It illustrates the level of drive and desire you need to get to the top—no matter what you're selling.

When I was in my early 20s, my younger brother, Dave, my Dad, and I owned a sports bar in suburban Detroit. I was already selling real estate by then—selling homes during the day and working in my bar at night until about 3 A.M. We called it the Overtime Saloon, which pretty well describes my work habits then. The whole family helped us out with it.

Anyway, I'll always remember our first day at the bar. We worked from 7 A.M. to 2:30 A.M.—and we took in less than $50 all day. It was pitiful. The mistake we made was a classic. We were waiting for the customers to come to us. We thought that by opening this great bar, people would just flock to us.

Well, they didn't. I learned that you should never wait for business to walk in your door. To be the best—heck, to be even moderately successful—you've got to go out and find your own customers.

As I said, I've always learned from my mistakes, and this was no exception. I remember turning to Dave and saying how we needed to hire some good bartenders to take over for us while we went out and found customers. Dave said something about we couldn't afford to do that. And I remember thinking and saying, "Hey, we can't afford *not* to do it!"

We started with simple stuff—basic marketing materials. We printed flyers and handed them out at softball games and in bowling alleys. Naturally we offered a lot of drink specials, pub food, happy hours, and the like—all the stuff that draws people into a sports bar.

We saw an immediate boost in our business. Most salespeople would have stopped there. But I wasn't satisfied. I didn't want just an ordinarily successful bar. I wanted the best sports bar in Detroit. I had big plans even then to buy lots of houses and be a real estate king. I believed that the income from the bar could help me achieve that goal.

So Dave and I bought a couple of used school buses and we began to go around to the local factory gates and shuttle the auto workers to the Overtime during their lunch breaks. It grew to be fabulously successful. Soon Chrysler Corp. was staggering the lunch hours of its factory workers so we could accommodate everyone. Pretty soon we were shuttling 1,000 factory workers a day to the Overtime this way.

I tried every marketing ploy I could think of to boost business. I put pretty waitresses on the buses to take orders. I installed CB radios on the buses so the customers could call in their orders in advance. Chrysler eventually got a little ticked at all the staggered schedules and offered to pay me not to run shuttle buses. I told them they probably couldn't afford to pay me enough to make up for the business I would lose.

We still had a few bad days. I remember once a bad snowstorm kept all our business away for the day. I still recall seeing all this food we had prepared and thinking, "What a waste."

But, mostly, it was gangbusters. Other bar owners in the area grew envious. Once a competing sports bar put out a flyer saying it would meet any drink special offered by the Overtime. Well, I wasn't going to sit still for it stealing my business. So I printed up a big sign that said "Three Drinks for $1." Then I loaded dozens of our customers onto buses and drove them over to this rival bar and I bought the drinks for everybody just so this bar would lose money trying to match our promotion. So this other bar owner and I came to a truce—we wouldn't try to steal each other's trade.

Well, before long that first $50 day had turned into $400 a day and then $4,000 a day. After a year or so a buyer came along and offered us $700,000 for the Overtime. The deal was for $300,000 down and monthly payments. He told us he'd keep us on to run the place. We agreed, but the day after we inked the deal he fired us. This guy didn't realize that what made the Overtime successful wasn't the drinks or the food but the marketing savvy that we brought to it.

A couple of months later, when he wasn't doing too well, he wanted to hire us back. But we told him no. We were too busy with our other ventures by then. But we did get the Overtime back when he couldn't keep up the payments. I eventually sold the Overtime four times, getting it back each time, until finally a nice Polish lady paid cash for it and wasn't susceptible to falling behind on payments.

I learned a lot at the Overtime—lessons about how to think of myself as a *marketer*, not a bartender. Lessons in how to be super-creative in devising marketing plans. Lessons in how to create my own customer base by doing what I had to do, like buying those old buses and installing CB radios on them.

Since then, I've created a thousand more marketing ideas to help grow my sales business. But I still think fondly of my days running the Overtime in my early 20s and all that I learned there about success.

RALPH'S RULE

There's no end to the success you can create if you remember to never stop thinking of new ways to market your product or service.

Disabilities Can't Stop You

In this chapter I want to tell you about one of the most inspirational men I know. In 1996, Stephen Hopson left his $300,000-a-year position as one of Merrill Lynch's top-producing stockbrokers in New York City. He's becoming a motivational speaker, and he's fast on his way to becoming a best-selling author. He reminds me every day that there are no limits to our success except those we place on ourselves.

Stephen Hopson is deaf—profoundly so, and he has been since his birth. After his parents discovered this when he was three years of age, they took him to doctors who gave them a stark choice. They could enroll Stephen in a special school for the deaf that would cater to his needs throughout childhood. Or they could mainstream him in the public school system and rely on the goodwill and limited expertise of ordinary teachers to deal with students who were deaf.

Well, Stephen's parents decided their son needed to interact with other kids who could hear so he could learn to function in a "hearing environment." They enrolled him in public school, and their choice had a profound effect on Stephen. Sure, he suffered at the hands of a few kids who made fun of him, but more importantly, he learned how to cope as an independent kid with friends and class work and relationships.

In high school, Stephen dreamed of being a champion swimmer. Try as he might, he couldn't make his body go fast enough in the water. In his last year of high school, he shaved all the hair from his body because he'd seen some Olympic swimmers on television who had done that. At the high school swimming championships, he sprang off the diving block like a cannon shot. He was one of the first swimmers to the first turn, then flipped over for the backstroke. He was really flying—so much so that he forgot to turn at the other end and crashed into the wall of the pool. Well, he didn't make the finals and so his dream didn't end with success, but many other dreams did.

When he got out of college, Stephen wanted to work on Wall Street. He dreamed of achieving riches as we all do. And he was no stranger to hard work. He was an impeccably groomed, highly intelligent, and motivated young man. But would that be enough? Stephen recalls how it took him months to convince a Merrill Lynch manager to take a chance on him. Finally the manager did—to his great good fortune, and to Stephen's.

Within three years, Stephen's initial production had soared 1,700 percent. He was competing against 12,000 financial consultants at the firm but consistently placed in the top 1,500 in sales contests. He won trips to Bermuda, Mexico, Florida, and other resort locations for his efforts. He also made Merrill Lynch's prestigious Executive Club for top salespeople three years in a row.

How did he do it? By using a lot of the tools I describe in this book: planning, visualization, embracing the latest technology, staying in touch with clients. In other words, he followed the basics and leveraged his natural talents to become one of the nation's top producers.

I think here I'll let Stephen tell some of his own story.

"Starting out, I realized I had to use unique ways to attract a client base, since cold-calling rarely worked for me. Cold-calling rarely works for anyone, but imagine trying to call someone through a relay service for the deaf, where the deaf person calls an 800 number using a TTY, a telephone device for the deaf that looks like a typewriter with a screen on it, and instructs the operator to call a person with a regular phone. The deaf caller types a message which is relayed by the operator to the person on the other end and his/her response is typed back to me. An ordinary conversation that might take you fifteen minutes would take me twice as long or longer. This method became even more complicated when the operator didn't type fast enough to keep up with the conversation.

"So, I had to get myself out and be seen. I went to community functions, parties, conventions, seminars. I spoke everywhere. In the beginning of my career I'd give investment seminars once or twice a month. In addition, I found ways to get my name in community newspapers with a photo if possible to establish credibility. Needless to say, marketing was the key to being seen. In 1995, my success caught the attention of CNN and my interview was wired all over the world for an entire weekend. Having faith, courage, and determination attracts unique opportunities far beyond your wildest dreams!

"Once I began to establish myself, I would try to stay in touch by phone. Fortunately, halfway through my career at Merrill Lynch the AT&T relay system adopted a fantastic new technology for deaf people who spoke articulately. This new method was called the 'voice carry over' or 'VCO' method. This was an exciting feature for an active, confident person like me. It worked this way. The deaf person would call the relay operator and request a 'VCO call to Mr. Smith.' The operator would switch to VCO mode, which enabled me to speak directly to Mr. Smith on the phone. This meant my clients would be able to hear my voice (which was especially important during times of turbulence in the markets, when they needed to hear my reassuring voice and not that of the operator!). When I was done talking, I would say 'go ahead' and the client would then respond through the operator, who would type it back to me. This method made my telephone calls at least halfway normal. When the VCO method arrived, I was excited because not only was I able to speak directly to my clients with my own voice but I was able to cut the time of my calls in half. Needless to say, my clients (and friends) loved it!

"An interesting note. Even though I was a deaf financial consultant, that did not mean that hard-of-hearing people flocked to me for advice. In fact, I had to work three times as hard to open new accounts with them! The reason it was harder to gain their trust was because deaf people historically had been taken advantage of so often that they all had horror stories about it. Probably 70 percent of my clients were of normal hearing.

"Eventually, I began to get referrals and stopped doing seminars because seminars were quite time consuming (from securing the space to sending out invitations and doing follow-ups before and after the seminars). I developed an effective system where I would send happy clients a letter asking for referrals. The letter would say something like, 'It's a wonderful honor and privilege to be serving your financial needs at this time. I have enjoyed helping your investments grow and would like to do the same for your friends, family, and associates. In order for me to continue serving your needs, I need to continue growing my business through your referrals. Please list those you think would benefit from my services.' This was the secret to getting referrals—asking all my satisfied clients. It was a safe, nonthreatening way of asking for help.

"After a few years, I was making more money than I ever thought I could. But I was experiencing a burning desire to do more. So at the end of 1996, I left my six-figure, award-winning career at Merrill Lynch to become a motivational speaker and author. Today, I'm working on a book that I know will be a best-seller. I'm looking forward to the book tour in 1999. My wildest dreams are coming true because I believed, dreamed, and had enormous faith!"

The book Stephen refers to here is the newest in the line of Chicken Soup for the Soul series, which have sold millions of copies around the world. The main author, Mark Victor Hansen, asked me a year ago to put together one of the books by, for, and about people with disabilities. Stephen is helping me with this and we'll take our book tour together when it comes out.

I'll tell you more about Stephen later on, but for now, remember his example of overcoming the odds. Next time you feel you can't win because of this or that factor against you, think of Stephen and try a little harder.

RALPH'S RULE
Success is not a matter of brains or beauty but of desire and hard work.

Know Your Product

My wife, Kathy, and I have been settled happily for the past several years in our dream house in metropolitan Detroit. We had it built to our special wants and needs. It has many rooms and a special place for my enormous collection of electric trains. When I had the photos taken for my personal brochures, I was photographed standing in the middle of this train set. There are computers for us and the kids and a beautiful entertainment center where, among other things, I display my collection of special edition bottles of bourbon, including one from Jack Daniel's they sent me after I wrote them a fan letter.

But here's my point. If we're putting down roots now, it wasn't always like that. During the first 20 years I spent in the real estate business, I moved about once a year. Twenty houses in 20 years. After I got married in 1985, I think I almost drove Kathy nuts with this practice. But I still believe it was absolutely necessary for me to move a lot. It taught me what was happening in my marketplace. Nothing else would have been such good training. I got to see houses the way my customers do—as a product that I might be moving into myself.

Getting to know your product and marketplace in this way is crucial. I don't care what you sell, I'm a firm believer that you have to know your own product or service. Not just have a general understanding of it, but know it inside and out. And that means you have to experience it firsthand. If you sell Corvettes, you better drive a Corvette. If you sell guitars, you ought to play guitars all the time.

Let me tell you about Patty Klein, a travel agent here in metro Detroit. Patty is president of Travel Education Institute, the oldest and largest trainer of travel agents in Michigan. She's a travel counselor herself with a company called A-Plus Travel. When I asked Patty what a good travel agent needs to do, she replied that a successful travel counselor first must be well-traveled.

"You have to know the destinations, cruise ships, and resorts you will be recommending," Patty says. Patty's been to over 50 different countries and sailed on more than 15 cruise ships. With this base of experience, Patty can recommend a cruise line or a hotel or a destination to a client and talk knowledgeably about it. Not many travel counselors have that kind of extensive product knowledge, but it's a key element of Patty's success.

It may be easier than you think to come by your expertise. When I was moving every year, I could often reduce the sales commission because I acted as my own Realtor. In Patty Klein's case, she can take advantage of steep discounts offered to agents by airlines, hotels, and so forth. Travel agents receive discounts such as 75 percent off coach airfare, 50 percent off hotels, and cruises for as little as $35 a day. They get these discounts so they can experience these travel options firsthand.

If you're in sales and you're not using your own product or service, you're making a major mistake.

By the way, Patty practices another of my recommendations, which is to not be shy about passing out business cards along the way.

"I met one of my best clients on an airplane from Miami coming back from a cruise," she says. "She travels a great deal and was impressed with my own travel experiences. Since that flight, based on my personal service for her, she has referred over 50 new clients to me. Similarly, I met a couple in line checking in for the same flight I was on to Manzanillo, Mexico. We chatted for a while, and I gave them a card. When we arrived home, they called me and booked a very nice Alaskan cruise and a tour to France."

RALPH'S RULE

You can't fake product knowledge, and your customers will detect your lack of expertise. To succeed in sales, you've got to know what you're selling. The only way to do that is to experience your marketplace firsthand. Not only should you get out there and sell, but you ought to get out there and buy, too.

The Art of Self-Promotion

These days, when just about everyone is leaping into the sales professions, the name of the game is separating yourself from the pack. You can do that with marketing and self-promotion. Of course, you also need a great deal of expertise, hard work, drive, and time-management skills. But if your potential customers don't know you're in business—if they don't sense that *you* are different from all those other salespeople they could turn to— then all the skills in the world won't help you.

If you think of some of the great brand identities in our culture—Coke, Nike, the Energizer Bunny, Wal-Mart—all these household names got that way through clear, persistent image and marketing campaigns. You can and must do the same for yourself if you want to rise to the top of the sales profession.

Our promotional messages distinguish us in a way that our products and services don't. Let's face it, one insurance policy operates about like the rest; one dental exam is about like another (assuming basic competence on the part of the dentist); and the same is more or less true for the products and services offered by mortgage brokers, financial planners, tax consultants, tree surgeons, computer consultants, caterers, long-distance phone resellers, and Realtors like me.

If our products are about the same, it's the little things we do that distinguish ourselves from our competition. Ultimately, they count for a lot. And of those little extras, nothing makes you stand out like a good promotional campaign.

I've always promoted myself, and I've always seen the results. Today my promotional efforts include a full-color personal brochure and a Web page. I also do all the usual things salespeople do, like sending out birthday cards to my clients and sending fruit baskets or turkeys on special occasions. I just do a lot more of it than other salespeople and I try to be more creative than others.

My efforts really took off a couple of years ago when I engaged the services of Hobbs/Herder Advertising, a California-based company that deals with professional service providers, particularly those in real estate. In fact, one of their creative people, Dennis LeBlanc, came up with the title of my first book. Greg Herder, the CEO, has since become a good friend. As Greg says, "Today's consumers want to feel as if they were the only customer on Earth." It's up to salespeople to give their customers that warm, fuzzy feeling. That starts with a personal marketing campaign that lets people know that we're there to serve them.

Let me give you some tips to guide your personal marketing campaign. I've developed these rules from years of trial and error with my own marketing and self-promotion campaigns. I've also gotten a lot of good ideas from experts like Greg Herder and from a slew of top-performing salespeople. I'm sure most or all of these will benefit you.

Separate Your Own Identity from That of Your Employer

Just as Kleenex has a brand identity separate from Kimberly-Clark and the Energizer Bunny exists in our minds independent of the Eveready Battery Company, we need to create our own distinct identities within our corporate sphere.

The answer is to produce your own marketing materials that stress your own identity and image. Sure, you'll also put your company's name on them. But if you want to make that all-important personal connection with your customers, you've got to make sure that *you* are the star of your marketing campaign. You're creating your own brand identity as distinct from your company as the Corvette is from General Motors.

Be Yourself!

"I think the biggest mistake that most people make in personal marketing is that it's not personal," says Greg Herder. "They think that slapping a name and a photo on something is personal marketing."

In fact, most of those "personal" brochures sent out by doctors and financial planners and Realtors are pretty anonymous. The photos are all the same size; they depict salespeople in the same pose, often with the same grin on each face. These look-alike campaigns all project a stereotypical business or professional person who cannot be distinguished from a thousand others.

My campaign is different. Developed with Hobbs/Herder, it really plays off my personality, which, it's fair to say, is upbeat, full of energy, and eager to be of service. So my brochure shows me thoroughly enjoying the good things in my life—playing with my elaborate set of model trains, conferencing with my terrific staff, and just plain enjoying life. We don't use any boring standard "head and shoulders" shots. When people see my personal brochure and later meet me, they feel as if they already know me.

By the way, make sure the "you" that's presented really is *you*. Recently, a friend of mine took my brochure, pasted photos of himself and his staff over my own, and sent it to me as a joke. Sometimes, though, salespeople erroneously do pretty much the same thing when they copy almost verbatim what another successful agent has done. My brochure works because it reflects *me*, but any attempt to create a carbon copy for somebody else just won't work.

In other words, if you're a warm, fuzzy sort of person, take photos and develop a campaign that plays off that. But if you're not warm and fuzzy—if you're rather hard-edged and all business—then *don't* take warm and fuzzy photos. Be true to yourself. Your customers will spot the difference anyway.

Be Consistent in Your Image and Campaign

Think of some of the great marketing images: The Energizer Bunny has been out there for years but still keeps going and going. Nike has made its "swoosh" logo so well-known that it no longer needs even to use its name in ads; just the logo will do. And the Maytag repairman has been around for a quarter century but still remains instantly identifiable.

You've got to do the same with your marketing materials. A really great campaign that you change every couple of years won't be as effective as a moderately good one that you use year in and year out.

Of course you may need to update your photo now and then. A good time to do this is when your photo no longer looks like you. Not long ago I lost 100 pounds and my customers no longer recognized me, so I knew it was time to change my photo.

But a new photo doesn't mean a whole new look or new image. So be careful how you design your campaign in the beginning. As Greg Herder counsels, if you can't be comfortable with a campaign theme for at least 10 years, you shouldn't use it at all.

Consistency also means that all the various pieces of your campaign must project the same image. Whether it's direct mail, business cards, billboards, newspaper ads, speeches, personal appearances, or anything else, your materials must fit together in a unified way to broadcast the image you want.

Good Marketing Stresses the Personal, Not the Factual

Many salespeople make the mistake of stressing their technical expertise in their marketing campaigns. You know the sort of thing: "Have closed more deals than any other salesperson" or "Consistently scores in top 5 percent of all salespeople." These salespeople don't seem to understand that a marketing campaign is designed only to get prospects to call you. Much of the technical information found in marketing materials, especially detailed product information, is better held until the sales call itself.

As Greg Herder says, "Until a consumer is face to face with you, they don't want to be educated." Rather, your campaign should be about persuading potential customers that you're someone they want to meet and get to know, someone who cares about them and shares their values.

Politicians are some of the best examples of personal marketing. If you look at successful presidential campaigns like President Clinton's 1992 effort, it was all personal. Clinton successfully stressed his "I feel your pain" and "I'm on your side" message. He left most or all of the details unsaid until after he got elected. It was a very shrewd, and highly successful, example of personal marketing.

By contrast, presidential candidates who stressed the purely technical or programmatic—people like Steve Forbes or the late Paul Tsongas—tended to suffer landslide defeats on Election Day.

RALPH'S RULE

Make sure your personal market is personal—that it really reflects you the person as well as you the salesperson—or it'll probably get lost amid all the other clutter.

More Thoughts on the Art of Self-Promotion

After I wrote that last chapter I found I still had a lot to say on self-promotion. So here are several more specifics to guide your efforts.

Spend, Spend, and Spend Some More

Today I spend more than $100,000 a year on my personal promotional efforts. That may seem like an astronomical amount to many of you. In fact, it may be more than your entire annual salary. My point is that while you can start small and work up to larger amounts, you absolutely must spend something on personal promotion to succeed.

Your investment in marketing and self-promotion will more than pay off its cost. Let me give you an example. A Realtor named Michael Davis, a salesperson with the RE/MAX-Realty Unlimited office in Brandon, Florida, went to Hobbs/Herder in 1995. He invested some $8,950 and received a personal brochure, print ads, direct mail pieces, Web pages, television commercials, letterhead, business cards, and a marketing strategy. Davis then paid $3,800 for 10,000 full-color brochures and another $3,800 for 50,000 oversized postcards. Including the fee to Hobbs/Herder, Davis has probably spent some $30,000 on personal marketing and self-promotion.

Did it do any good? In the two years since Davis rejuvenated his marketing campaign, his annual gross sales volume soared from $6 million to $11 million. The extra commissions generated by those sales amounted to some $350,000. It didn't all go to Davis, of course; much of the increase is split with other agents. Yet it shows just how powerful a good personal marketing campaign can be.

Hobbs/Herder recommends that salespeople spend 15 to 30 percent of their gross dollar incomes on personal marketing. It's a fairly substantial amount, but look at it this way: Companies like Procter & Gamble and Nike each year spend at least that much of every dollar they take in on advertising. And their profit margins are enormous.

The research shows that the more you spend on marketing relative to your competition, the higher profit margin you have. I know that spending 30 percent of your gross on marketing when you make only $30,000 a year can be daunting. But you've got to look at it as a basic capital cost of doing business. It's the only thing that will separate you from the rest.

Once You've Got Your Marketing Materials, Use Them!

Having spent, say, $5,000 on full-color personal brochures, many salespeople are reluctant to give them away. These misguided salespeople believe that their brochures cost so much that they need to be hoarded for special occasions.

On the contrary, you need to give them away to everyone and anyone. I personally hand out thousands of brochures myself each year. I give them to waitresses and toll collectors on the highway and people I meet casually in restaurants. My office sends out a few thousand more each year. I know that one good commission will more than pay for the entire campaign. And I'm confident that if I get my brochure in enough hands I'll have more than one new sale.

Don't Be So Taken with One Format That You Stick with It When It Flops

I used to be a big fan of those refrigerator magnets that most salespeople like to give out. You know what I mean, the ones with our name and face and phone number on them. I even had my own technique. When I showed up at a customer's house for a presentation, I would walk directly into the kitchen and put my magnet on the refrigerator myself.

Today I no longer believe those magnets do any good at all. Every home I've ever been in has several of those magnets holding up pieces of paper in the kitchen. But do the customers ever call the salespeople who gave them those magnets? In my opinion, no. Today I believe that customers call us because we've projected a much more sophisticated image of a caring, sympathetic person who shares their values. You can't get that across with a silly magnet. You need a more thoughtful campaign to succeed.

Take my word for it. Dump your magnets, and put your promotional dollars into a good personal brochure instead.

Use Cable Television

Here's one specific placement tip from Greg Herder. Place your ads on cable television. "Almost any budget can afford local commercial time on top national stations," he says of cable. "It's like adding rocket fuel to a local marketing campaign."

Reprints Can Be Your Best Friend

Whenever you're quoted in a newspaper or magazine article, get reprints. Pay for a good full-color reproduction. Send out copies in direct mail to your entire customer base. Use the same photo that ran with the article or import a better photo. Go to a fair amount of trouble to get your reprint looking just right. It's less expensive than you may think and it'll do you a lot of good. Reprints can be even more important than the original article because you can target the audience you want to see it.

Don't Put All Your Eggs in a Single Marketing Basket

As I've said, I hand out thousands of personal brochures. But I also do direct mail, a Web page, newspaper advertisements, and many other forms of marketing and self-promotion. That way, if one thing doesn't work, something else will.

RALPH'S RULE
Market yourself, market yourself, and then market yourself some more!

Seeing Business Where It Isn't

I believe one reason I'm so successful is that I can spot a sale where most salespeople wouldn't even look. This is a critical skill to develop. The best salespeople will always see opportunities where others don't. The average salesperson will do a lot of the usual things and accept a certain level of success. But the really aggressive and creative salesperson literally will make things happen.

For example, recently I was working with a couple who were going through a divorce. This is sadly a typical situation today. Like many other couples, this one had a lot of debt and their only large asset was their home. In most cases, a salesperson would have just sold the home and the couple would have split the proceeds. But in this case, the wife still wanted to live in the house even though the husband wanted to sell it and get his money.

Complicating things even more was their credit card debt, which cost them about $800 a month in minimum payments.

Well, I looked over their situation and found that mortgage rates had come down considerably since they bought their home. So I got them to refinance at my mortgage company. This saved them hundreds of dollars a month in mortgage payments. This refinancing generated enough leeway to ease the burden of the credit card payments and still cash out some of the equity for the husband.

My company now has a whole system for helping divorced couples get clear of their homes and split the assets as smoothly as possible. We try to be creative in how we do this so that the husband and wife will each come out feeling they've been treated fairly and, we hope, come back to us again when they need more real estate help.

We've also developed an entire system for working with people going through foreclosure. This is a terrible situation for the people going through it, and we often find that the husband and wife are lying to each other about the depth of the situation. But something like 4 percent of all the homeowners in America are behind on their payments, so it may help to know that you're not alone if you're going through this. Heck, even I lost one of the first homes I ever owned to foreclosure back some 20 years ago. I describe this traumatic situation, and the lessons I learned from it, in *Walk Like a Giant, Sell Like a Madman*. In trying to help others through this difficult period, I've set up an entire system in my office to work with people. They may lose their home, but often we can work with people to let them still live in the home and make rental payments to us with an option of buying back the home when they recover financially.

We also have a whole system in place for helping investors buy up vacant homes that were taken back by either the Veterans Administration or HUD when the owners defaulted on a mortgage. This is an excellent way to become an investor because you can buy these properties for little or no down payment. Often these homes are in disrepair. My investors will buy them, fix them up, and either rent them or resell them quickly.

This is the kind of business that many a Realtor would avoid because it seems too complicated. But, to me, it's just another way of serving the public and generating transactions to help my bottom line.

The late Ben Feldman, the most famous life insurance salesman in history, used to sell more life insurance than anybody by inventing new reasons for people to buy it. When Feldman started selling life insurance in the 1930s, people bought it mainly to replace the lost wages of a husband who died young. Feldman began to pitch the idea of buying insurance to cover estate taxes. "A man walks out and the tax man walks in," he'd say, or, "It takes a man years to build up his wealth and it takes the tax man just a day to take it all." Or he'd show a customer two checks, one tiny one written to his insurance firm and one enormous one written to the IRS. And he'd tell the customer he could write the first check today or his heirs could write the second one after his death. These reasons convinced thousands of customers that Feldman was right.

In all these cases I'm describing—customers with bad credit, customers with problems that seem unsolvable, customers who think they have no need for your product—an ordinary salesperson will walk away and go look for the easy sale somewhere else. But the extraordinary salesperson will see opportunity where others don't. By now a significant chunk of my business each year comes from these nontraditional sources, including my foreclosure work and working with investors and working with divorcing couples. I attribute much of my success today to my ability to creatively see business where it has never existed before.

RALPH'S RULE

Not only should you get creative about looking for unusual sales opportunities, but you should get systematic about it, too. If you uncover one opportunity for a nontraditional sale, chances are there are a multitude of others just like it. Develop a system to reach these customers.

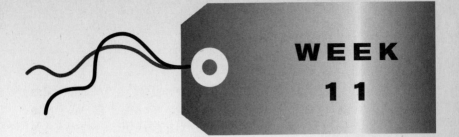

Problem Solving with Your Staff

Let me tell you a story about a creative solution to a serious problem.

About a year ago as I write this, I started Summit Title, my own title company. Since every real estate transaction involves a title search, and since I do more transactions than any other Realtor, I thought this would be a natural extension of my brokerage work. I studied the market and went out and hired a good staff and a great manager, Mary Shamo, a top salesperson in her own right.

Well, we had a great opening month and I thought I was a genius. Then the slide began. The problem is that our company wasn't yet well established. We had no customer base to go back to and many of our new salespeople were inexperienced. We didn't have enough cash coming in to cover overhead, and pretty soon I realized I had a serious problem on my hands.

I talked to my in-house lawyer, Peter Allen, who had helped me start Summit Title, and we went back and forth over whether we ought to close it down at once or try something else. I hated the idea of closing it. It was one of my babies, my pet projects, and I really believed that it would work. But I couldn't ignore the red ink, either, so we discussed how best to cut back without gutting the operation.

Rumors got around the staff and Mary came to me and said her staff wouldn't agree to take 20 percent pay cuts. I told her I didn't expect them to, but that some cutbacks were probably necessary. We just hadn't figured out what yet. A couple of hours later, Mary returned to my office. "Ralph," she said, "instead of laying off people, fire me. Don't pay me this big administrative salary. I'll become a salesperson."

I said something like, "Mary, you've got to be kidding. You're supposed to run the show." And she said, "Who's the best salesman on the team? I am, right?" And I had to admit that she was right.

Well, I went home and talked to Kathy, my wife, who actually is the owner of the business. She agreed with Mary. "You're job isn't to micromanage these operations, Ralph," she told me. "That's what you have managers for—to manage."

So the solution to our start-up problems at Summit Title was to let our manager quit and come back as a salesperson. She's happier doing deals again (and actually earning more money in commissions again than she earned in salary as a manager). We trimmed our costs substantially, and we were able to save the firm. With this breathing room, Summit Title had a chance to establish itself and now is doing quite well. So thank you, Mary, for giving up your job to save the jobs of others and to save my newest company.

I think this story illustrates several points about problem solving around the office. Everyone knows you have to "think outside the box." But how many of us actually do it? In this case, we had two guys with years of experience—me and my lawyer, Peter—basically coming up with the same old solution—cut costs by firing people or shutting the operation down. What an uncreative way to look at the problem! It took Mary and Kathy to come up with a much more creative solution. It was so good it worked out better for all of us.

So here's a list of reminders to help you with your office problem solving.

Ask for Help

Not one of us is as smart as all of us together. In this case, I didn't even ask for Mary's help; she more or less volunteered the solution to me. But I'm glad she did. Remember, if the problem concerns everyone, then everyone should be part of the solution.

For sure, I know how salespeople hate to give up any control. Many of you may be thinking you'd never ask for help. But you must. Assuming the staff you've assembled is as smart and talented as you think they are, don't neglect this amazing resource you have.

Don't Get Hung Up on Hierarchy

Along with asking for help, remember to think beyond the normal lines of authority. Department heads aren't the only ones with good ideas. In fact, often it's the people further down the line, the ones who are closer to the problem, who may know best how to solve difficult issues.

Foster a Problem-Solving Atmosphere

In my office, I try to delegate as much as possible. I try to create systems to handle volumes of work, and then I delegate to others as much as possible the running of these systems. I often tell people not to involve me in minor details or everyday problem solving. For one thing, I need to stay upbeat and focused on my main job—selling—and I can't afford to get caught in a trap of negativity over minor problems. But, beyond this, I like to let other people get creative in their daily jobs. The solutions tend to be better, and the employees happier, than if I'm trying to micromanage all the time.

Think Ends, Not Means

Many of the arguments we have around the office really concern means, not ends. Everyone wants to succeed and make money. But it's surprising how often we disagree on how. To the extent that I can, I try to hear someone's argument in terms of the end result, not whether I happen to agree with his immediate focus. If he gets to where I want him to go but along a different path than I would take, it can still be okay.

There are all kinds of reasons that we get caught up in unproductive problem solving. Maybe it's ego, or a fear of delegating, or a dozen other things. But if you involve others in your search for answers and get beyond those simplistic solutions that are generally ineffective or just plain wrong, you'll be surprised at the results.

RALPH'S RULE

Just as you train to make presentations, you have to train yourself to think creatively to solve problems. Begin today. It's a skill well worth acquiring.

Train Your Assistants Properly

A year ago I hired a young man named Paul Corona to work with me as an assistant. He's one of many helpers I've hired over the years. Twenty-some years ago, when I was just a green kid starting out in sales, I hired a high school student to answer phones for me after school. I still remember what a relief it was to have her handle the routine calls while I concentrated on doing what I do best—working with my buyers and sellers.

Pretty soon I added a secretary. Later I hired an assistant to handle my investment properties and another to help me with my closings. In time I delegated big chunks of my operation to assistants—marketing specialists, an in-house lawyer, my own CPA, and many, many more. These people represent my attempt to duplicate myself so that I can do even more. Believe me, there's no way I could handle the volume I do without my dedi-cated group of assistants.

Over the years, I've refined my way of training my assistants. That's what I want to talk about in this chapter. By now, I take it as a given that you're either a top salesperson or on your way to becoming one. So you probably know the importance of delegating routine work to others. What you may not realize is the importance of properly training your assistants. Correct training can make all the difference.

All too often, salespeople get no training at all. Typical is the experience of a friend in the insurance business. His boss showed him to a desk, on which sat a telephone and a phone book. The "training" consisted of listening to a cassette tape of instructions. My friend remembers that the tape kept jamming, so he had to take his ball-point pen to advance the tape past the sticky spots. And he remembers that the ceiling was rotten above the table and bits of dust and debris would fall now and then onto the table.

This scenario, unfortunately, is all too common even today. A newcomer is expected to learn the ropes entirely by cold-calling potential clients. Sometimes the training is a little better, but not much.

The average salesperson who hires an assistant is making a big breakthrough to greater wealth. But almost always you miss much of your potential bonanza by not training your assistants properly. Probably you just turn over the new assistant to somebody else to train. And the training consists mostly of technical matters—say, how to use a particular software program. What is entirely lack-ing—yet what I believe is so essential to our success—is training that teaches the spirit and mission of a sales team.

I've always understood that an assistant can help me only if he or she understands me and my philosophy and my driving ambition to succeed. Over the years, I've taken an ever increasing amount of time and trouble to train my assistants.

Today I make sure that my training plan includes having a new assistant shadow me for a period of time to better understand my business. I'll have my assistant simply hang out with me for a while. This helps the assistants see where they'll fit into the larger picture once they actually start work. In the old days that meant hanging with me for a day. Today, it's a much longer period of time.

This process reached something of a pinnacle a year ago when I hired Paul. I had known Paul for probably five years before he came to work for me. Now 31, Paul had spent a few years in sales in his early 20s in the medical supplies field. Then he got involved managing a family-owned restaurant. He spent almost six years doing that. I met him at the restaurant and used to chat with him when I'd go in for dinner. I learned that Paul was hardworking and ambitious but that he felt confined by his restaurant job. Often he had to work six nights a week until 3 A.M. He made pretty good money—often around $50,000 a year—but saw little hope of ever going beyond that. I saw that Paul had ambitions to achieve much greater success. I knew that he saw the sales profession as his means of doing that.

Eventually, both Paul and I were ready to make a deal. I offered him a position with my company and he accepted. Neither of us was sure exactly where he'd fit in yet. After all, my company now includes so many aspects, from buying and selling homes to developing condominium projects to managing investment property to offering mortgages and title insurance, that Paul could have fit in anywhere. Before we decided where, I wanted him to get a taste of what my business was all about.

So I had Paul do nothing but shadow me for a full 30 days. I paid him a salary during this time, because he wouldn't have any commissions coming in yet. He was with me all day and well into the evenings. He was there when I met with buyers and sellers, and he was there when I met with my personal attorney and my stockbroker. He accompanied me to my networking groups and when I saw my banker about getting money to develop land.

Paul's very first day on the job, I flew him to New Orleans to join me at a four-day real estate convention. I wanted him to attend the training seminars, but I also wanted him to get a better sense of who I am and my place in the sales world. Paul came back from New Orleans impressed both with what he had learned and with how much effort I was willing to put into his professional development.

As Paul himself says now, "What Ralph did for me was show me success during those 30 days. I saw people making money. I thought that with my personality and my willingness to work I could share in that success and bring in more. It definitely was a motivational thing."

Not only did I sell Paul on my company and my industry, but, as he puts it, "Ralph sold me on myself, too, and the possibility of my own success. I came home every day having seen something new and being excited about something else."

Did my elaborate training actually result in Paul's success? You be the judge. At the end of 30 days, we mutually decided that Paul would serve as one of my buyer's agents, that is, a salesperson who works with families trying to buy a home. Within 60 days of starting work as a buyer's agent, Paul had closed eight deals. In other words, he'd already matched the average annual production level of the typical Realtor in America. In his first year, Paul closed 43 transactions. Hiring Paul was one of the best moves I've made recently. I'm confident that he's going to make a lot of money for us both.

Now, I knew that Paul was something special when I met him. This personable, well-groomed young man was marked for success. But I still think my elaborate training system helped him. It indoctrinated Paul in the philosophy of my company, which involves hard work, service to customers, a commitment to financial success, and a driving need to never be beaten by our competitors. Paul probably would have succeeded in time anyway. But those first 30 days jump-started his career in a way nothing else could.

That's the message I want you to take away from this chapter. Your assistants ought to be much more than envelope stuffers and phone answerers. Your assistants are extensions of yourself. They are there to relieve you of the matters others can handle. They free you to do only those tasks that you as a top sales producer must do. You've got to make their hiring and training one of your highest priorities.

One helpful way to envision this is to think of your assistants as profit centers. Paul is a profit center who works with buyers. I have other assistants who work with sellers. I have others who help me with closings and others who help me with marketing and public relations. My marketing assistants do much more than write press releases for me. They handle the selling of my motivational tapes and other educational products that I produce. I can justify each and every assistant on my payroll based on the extra profit they bring into my firm.

Remember the words of my friend Monica Reynolds, one of the best sales trainers in the nation. "If your assistants are not an asset, they're a liability." That's so true. You need to fire them up or fire them. And the best way to fire them up is to train them right in the first place.

RALPH'S RULE

Training an assistant must cover much more than mere technical aspects like how to use a software program. It must cover a spectrum of emotional and motivational topics, too. Don't ignore these "soft" sides of training. Ultimately these factors will spell success for your new assistant and for you.

Meet "Little Ralph"

About a year ago I met a bank administrator named Craig Peltier. Craig was in charge of the back-office operation at my bank. He kept the paper flow moving and the staff productive. Customers didn't see him much because he operated behind the scenes. But, as any banker or any salesperson knows, such people are invaluable for keeping the operation running smoothly.

Well, anyway, I'm in the bank a lot, not only dealing with my own accounts but talking to lenders about lines of credit and that sort of thing. As time went by, I met Craig and got to know him. He impressed me as a steady, hardworking professional. And one day I offered him a job at my firm.

Initially, Craig came over to run the administrative side of my new title company. But eventually I brought him upstairs, gave him the title of assistant vice president, and made him my right-hand man. After that, Craig went with me everywhere. He attended all my meetings with clients. He sat in on every conference with bankers and other lenders. He monitored my schedule. He kept track of staff developments.

But, most important, Craig was the ultimate detail person. As he put it, "I kept the promises Ralph made. I followed up on everything he said. When he promised a customer that we'd do something, I made sure it got done."

I've always employed assistants to help me, ever since I started in the sales business right after high school. I guess in a way Craig was one of my ultimate assistants. I often describe hiring an assistant as a way to duplicate yourself. Well, in hiring Craig I did just that. The staff even began referring to him sometimes as "Little Ralph," because he became so important to me.

Every salesperson needs to hire one or more assistants. You'll know the time has come when you can't fulfill your promises; when you find work getting lost instead of getting done; when your family never sees you; when the administrative side of your sales business threatens to overwhelm you. We salespeople, you know, really aren't such great detail people, no matter how many details we must keep track of. We're the emotional ones who do the deals. We create bridges for buyers and sellers to cross. Mostly we leave the details to others, or at least we should. No one else can do what we can do. No one else can build the bridges like we can.

That's why you need one or more assistants. And that's why, at my level of production, I finally needed an assistant like Craig. I've already got dozens of people working for me—helping me with listings, with closings, with buyers and sellers, with public relations and marketing, setting up interviews and listening to customers. But I finally needed someone who could just follow me around and keep track of all the things that I deal with every single day.

And what sort of person fits this job? Certainly not another salesperson. Craig is a rather laid-back kind of guy, reserved, quiet, and even-tempered. Unruffled would be a good word. He had to be. If he had the personality I do, we probably would never have worked well as a team. We'd have been bouncing off each other's egos. But given that he was a perfect complement to my high-energy, supercharged personality, Craig was a great match.

Unfortunately, Craig eventually decided that he wanted to get back into the banking industry and he ended up leaving me. But, as difficult as it was to lose Craig, there is a lesson to be learned in his leaving. The better someone is, the more they will be recruited by other companies. I stole Craig from my bank and another bank stole Craig from me.

Fortunately, as Craig became more valuable to my operation, the more I cross-trained others to handle his work. I'm sure you've heard the saying "Don't put all of your eggs in one basket." Well, that saying applies to your business. The more responsibilities someone has, the more important it is to make sure others know how to handle those responsibilities. Unfortunately, people have accidents, leave jobs and take vacations all the time. It's up to you to make sure that one person doesn't have the ability to shut down your entire business by leaving or becoming incapacitated.

For most salespeople, it may be quite a while before you become so busy you need someone like Craig to follow your every move. More likely, first you'll hire your own secretary or other staff assistant. As you go along, you'll add others to help you with various aspects of your business. But never try to go it alone. When the details begin to slip and you find yourself losing control of important situations because you're too busy, hiring an assistant is the way to stay on target.

RALPH'S RULE

If you don't have an assistant, you are one. That is, if you don't have someone handling the routine chores around the office, then you're wasting your valuable selling time on mundane details.

Six Ways to Write Better Notes to Your Customers

Most salespeople send little thank-you notes and Christmas cards to their customers. It's a nice way to stay in touch, and it keeps your name in front of your clients. Unfortunately, most of these greetings are utterly routine—the same boring Christmas cards and the same impersonal thank-you notes that every sales-person sends. Most wind up in the garbage without a second thought.

Over the years, I've developed a unique mailing strategy to the point where it's an important marketing tool for me. I want my mailings to send a message that I'm an informed, concerned salesperson—someone who really cares about my customer's well-being. That may sound like a tall order, but here are six ways that you can elevate your mailings above the routine.

1. Don't send cards on the same holidays everyone else does. Everybody sends Christmas cards and birthday cards. I don't like to get lost in the pack. I send cards to my customers on less traditional holidays, like the Fourth of July instead of Christmas. I've even sent out cards on Groundhog Day. Few, if any, other salespeople remember these occasions, so I really stand out when I do. By the way, I'd like to credit my friend Stanley Mills, one of the top Realtors in Tennessee, for teaching me this technique.

2. Send a note even when you don't get the sale. We all send thank-you notes when we close a deal. (At least I hope you're all doing that by now!) But I will often send out a note even when the deal falls through. I just want customers to know that I'm still in the market and that I will be for many years to come. You never know. Someday they'll need the services of a salesperson again. Often, the deal they've inked with somebody else falls through, and in those cases, I'm usually the first one they call simply because I've gone to so much trouble to stay in touch with them.

3. Send a note when you've been quoted in the news media. I take a lot of time to organize my press clips. I like to send out copies by the thousands. Often I'll scribble a little note that says, "Thought you might be interested in this issue." Many of your competitors will send out simple thank-you notes, but hardly any of them will send a copy of a press clip. It's another way to help you stand out from the pack.

4. Send a note after you've met someone new. We're constantly meeting new people, and I always carry around marketing materials with me to give them. I hand out a couple thousand of my personal brochures a year to all sorts of people—waitresses, valet car parkers, people I meet at weddings and funerals. If, for some reason, I can't give something to them right away, I'll ask for a business card from them and send something to their home or office. Remember, a salesperson succeeds in direct proportion to the number of people who know him. Even if your new acquaintance doesn't seem like an immediate prospect, you never know. They may turn into prospects later. As I've said before, sooner or later everyone needs a car, a home, a computer, clothes, or whatever it is you sell.

5. Send mail as a way to generate different kinds of income streams. In my office, we've developed a multitude of products that have proven helpful to both my customers and other salespeople. For customers, these include reports on "How to Ready Your Home for Sale" or "How to Buy a House with No Down Payment." For salespeople, I generate training tapes and publications like "The 10 Biggest Mistakes I've Ever Made," outlining how I've turned each of my errors into a winning strategy. Many of my mailings include information on how to buy these products. So the mailing accomplishes two things. It keeps my name before the public, and it generates enormous income, too.

6. Send out lots of different kinds of mailings. As I've been saying, my mailings to customers include thank-you notes, birthday cards, press clippings, holiday greetings, follow-ups on previous contacts, and a whole lot more. You can turn almost anything into an occasion for a mailing. In my office, we mass mail an entire marketplace every month or so. It computes to hundreds of thousands of pieces of mail per year. But it's all worth it, because by now I'm the best-known salesperson in my market. When people think of buying or selling a home, I'm the one they think of first.

And here's one more hint. With all the good contact-management software on the market today, generating mail for your customers can be as easy as tapping a keyboard. Don't pass up this outstanding way to stay in touch with your market.

RALPH'S RULE

Just because most other salespeople use a certain technique doesn't mean you can't find a unique version of your very own. Try it!

The Importance of Mentors

My job is more than my job. It's my passion, but it's also my hobby. People say, "What do you do for a hobby?" Well, Saturday and Sunday, even if I'm with my family, I might want to drive by a few pieces of real estate just to see what they're like. I think if I sold cars, I'd want to drive around and look at cars. If I sold computers, I'd want to know about all the latest computers. I think the passion, the hobby, comes into play there.

One way to nurture this passion, especially early in your career, is through mentors. A mentor is any person who helps you understand something about yourself and your business. It doesn't have to be a boss necessarily; it can be an inspirational speaker like Zig Ziglar or a relative who showed you the way.

My original mentors were my parents, even though I didn't follow in my dad's footsteps as a builder. What I learned from my parents was work. My parents would not let me have a paper route because they wanted me to have time for school, but on Saturdays and Sundays, I could go to work for my dad. I'd be there all the time. He's retired now, but he still works every single day. I learned from my parents that hard work pays off.

Probably more important than the hard work, what I learned from my parents was the importance of doing things for others. My mom would do anything to help someone. I know they helped put people through college and buy cars. I remember my parents would give when they didn't even have it to give. I learned that from them, and today I give a significant part of my time and earnings to charitable affairs. You've got to give something back.

I think I must have gotten my passion for selling from my grandmother. My grandparents came to Detroit from Kentucky in the 1930s so my grandfather could work in the auto industry here. Once my grandfather got fired for smoking on the job. But, because the auto industry was booming, he was able to get hired at another plant right away. At first, they lived with a few other families in a house in Detroit.

Growing up, my brothers and I were very close with my grandparents. We were so close with my mother's parents that we called them Mom and Dad. We called my parents Mommy and Daddy. Today, we call my mom Mother, and we call my dad the Boss. It was almost like having two sets of parents. Eventually, my grandparents and my family lived across the street from each other. My grandparents also had some property and raised some ponies. Sometimes after school, we would go over to their house to ride the ponies. It was a really neat situation.

When I was a toddler, my grandmother started a jewelry business. She sold costume jewelry under the name Fashion Treasures. I really enjoyed being around her selling parties—I liked being around all the people. They tell me stories now, how the phone would ring and I'd be soaking in the bathtub which was right down the hall. I'd jump out of the tub, run down the hallway, grab a piece of paper and pencil and say, "It's jewelry business, I'll get it!" There are even some photos of me doing this, naked and wet.

Another mentor I can remember was named Frank Gardner. I worked in his gas station. I would work after school; ultimately I was the manager. He was just a great guy. I learned how to deal with people from him.

For example, I and another guy who worked there had our girlfriends come over in the summer. It was warm, and we were washing and waxing our cars in the two bays in the gas station. I remember Frank and his wife went out to dinner that night. I didn't think there'd be any problems. If people came in for gas, we'd hurry out and take care of them.

Well, I remember Frank pulling up, and from the look on his face I knew he wasn't happy. He came in, took his tie and jacket off. He helped us dry both these cars. Then he asked us to move the cars out, and he asked me to come into his office because I was the one in charge. When we went into his office, Frank asked me, "What do you think you did wrong?"

I said, "We shouldn't have been washing our cars when we were working for you, Frank."

He said, "No, that's not what you did wrong. Sometimes there's nothing to do; you've got all your work done. What you did wrong was you were doing two cars at the same time, and both of my stalls were full. If somebody drove by and wanted an oil change or a tire fixed, they would think I'm busy and would go to another station. I don't mind you working on your own vehicles, but at least the customers should know that they could pull up here and you could take care of them."

Well, Frank could have fired me, but he didn't. Instead, he taught me a lesson about business and how to treat people. He could have yelled at me, but the way he corrected me, I learned a lot. It's in me forever.

RALPH'S RULE

Mentors come in all varieties, from relatives and friends to bosses and coworkers. If you don't have anyone helping you right now, make it your business to find some. You can learn so much from the right person.

Work Your Priorities

Earlier in this book we met Stephen Hopson, the dedicated young man who overcame his deafness to pull down $300,000 a year at Merrill Lynch. When I got to know him, I was curious how he went about his daily work as a stockbroker. Although I have my own systems in place for setting goals, making calls, and handling paperwork, I was curious to see if Stephen's deafness imposed any special requirements on him during the course of the normal working day.

The answer was surprisingly few. Aside from the special VCO telephone technology required, Stephen pretty much went about his day just like you or me or any other top producer. He networked. He called past customers. He asked for referrals. He wrote down his goals and planned his day around achieving them.

Perhaps most of all, Stephen prioritized. How many times have you heard that you're supposed to do "first things first"? Probably a million. But how many salespeople get sidetracked every day with frivolous errands, nonproductive calls, and administrative trivia? Far too many. Even a top performer like me has to guard against these kinds of time-wasters. I don't always succeed entirely, but I think we concentrate better than almost anyone on those tasks that are most important.

How to do this? Well, let's start by having Stephen tell us about his method at Merrill Lynch.

"The clients I approached first were always the top 20 clients that produced 80 percent of my business. I called these top 20 clients almost every day to keep them informed about market conditions. They were most active in the investment decision-making process and followed my advice without the usual delaying tactics, like 'Let me speak to my wife, son, daughter, lawyer, mother, father, sister, etc.' It helped that they were decisive! Dealing with these kinds of clients made my job a bit easier. They were wealthy businessmen, doctors, lawyers, business owners, socialites, etc. They were busy people and for them time was at a premium (as was mine), so we respected each other's time on the telephone. We often kept our telephone conversations quick, brief, and to the point. I rarely 'chatted' with clients. Chatting was reserved for in-person appointments over breakfast, lunch, dinner, or coffee."

Once Stephen took care of his most productive clients, he would then work his way down the list of his remaining customers. "On average," he says, "*all* my clients heard from me at least once a month either by telephone, fax, a letter, a short note, or an e-mail. Communication was absolutely essential."

Prioritizing around your top 20 clients is just one way to focus. There are many others.

Another salesperson I know divides his clients into A, B, and C piles. He works the A clients first and hardest. These are the ones who produce the most business, either directly or by referrals. Only when the A list has been serviced does he turn to the B list. These are lesser prospects that with a little work might become A prospects one day. The C list is mostly the "discard pile"—those clients or deals that produce either so little profit or so much trouble that they're better off going elsewhere.

Here's another technique. Several years ago, when I first met my friend Allan Domb, the condominium king of Philadelphia, I was impressed by his ability to make 100 phone calls a day. But I was even more impressed by his ability to rank all these calls in order of importance. Allan notes what each call will be worth to him in dollars. For example, if call A succeeds, it will be worth $1,000 to him; call B might be worth $500; and call C will produce only $50 for him. Naturally, Allen works the A call first, then the B, and finally the C.

Simple as these techniques sound, they have been absolutely essential to the success of these salespeople. This sort of prioritizing is as basic as when your mother told you to do your homework before you went out to play. You do the difficult or the important stuff first, and the rest is easy. On the other hand, if you don't take care of your most important clients first, when will you have time to catch up with them later on? Again, we all know this—but millions of salespeople, and millions more people in other walks of life, still ignore this need. Maybe we should listen to Mom more often!

There are many useful ways of prioritizing your daily tasks. The novelist Elmore Leonard used to juggle his book writing with a daytime job at an advertising agency. He'd get up at 5 A.M., work on his latest novel for a couple of hours, and then go to work at the ad agency. Eventually, he became successful enough to chuck the day job and concentrate full-time on his writing. But while he was doing both, getting his writing done early was his way of doing the most important job first.

Whether you use an A, B, C rating, or assign a dollar amount to each task, or make a list of your 20 top clients, you'll have to develop some system. Without one, you'll have no way to judge your progress.

RALPH'S RULE

We salespeople face an overwhelming number of tasks each day. Do the important stuff first. It sounds simple, but you'd be surprised how many people ignore this basic advice.

Keeping Your Past Customers

The National Automobile Dealers Association estimates that, in a lifetime, a repeat customer can be worth more than $300,000 to a dealership. Contrast that with the one-time customer who spends $15,000 or $20,000 at a dealership and never returns. Which type of customer would you rather have?

I've made this point many times but it bears repeating. I would rather deal with a past customer or get a referral from a past customer than deal with a new customer who walks in my door. The past customer is always more valuable. He or she represents not just that one sale but a stream of income over many years.

Many salespeople rob themselves of this loyal customer base in a variety of dumb, silly ways. If I could do one thing in this book, it would be to get you to correct this obvious mistake.

Here are a few things to keep in mind:

Remember That You're Building a Relationship, Not Making a Sale

Many customers would rather get a root canal than buy a new car or talk to a Realtor or listen to a sales presentation of any kind. That's because many salespeople still practice a slick-talking style of presentation. You just know the salesperson's goal is to separate you from your money before you leave. No wonder the customer gets turned off.

But in these competitive times, we no longer have the option to treat customers as one-time targets whom we'll never see again. The bad salespeople simply won't survive. General Motors, Ford, and Chrysler are downsizing the number of their dealerships to create a more streamlined sales organization. Hundreds of dealerships will close in the next couple of years. That means that thousands of salespeople will be out of work. In my business, trends like computerization, consolidation of agencies by national firms, and other factors mean that only about half the 600,000 active Realtors will still be in business by the early 21st century. In this tough, competitive world, only the smartest salespeople will survive.

In every business I know, developing relationships with clients is more important than getting a one-time sale. A good restaurant may do two-thirds of its business from people who have dined there at least once before. A good advertising salesperson will return to the same ad buyers time after time. Even a good baby-sitter will establish a relationship with a few families, rather than working for a different family every single time.

When you meet a potential client for the first time, ask yourself how you can help solve this customer's long-term needs, not how you can rack up another sale at that moment.

Learn What Personal Service Really Means

The very finest hotels, like the Ritz Carlton, or the finest shops, like Tiffany & Co., practice a brand of service that goes beyond what a customer expects. Once, for example, I wanted to buy my father a miniature golf club at Tiffany's. I had procrastinated about ordering it until it was too late to get it engraved for his birthday. Well, I thought I'd buy the club anyway and give it to him later, but the sales representative not only put a rush on to get the club ASAP, but she also personally wrote a note to my dad to explain that it was the store's fault and not mine that it wasn't engraved. That, believe me, was well beyond anything I had expected.

At the Ritz Carlton, service training includes knowing the guest's name, making eye contact, having someone there when they first pull up at your door. (Interestingly, many successful midmarket companies like Wal-Mart also use this same "greeter" concept to welcome customers). Service includes keeping track of a guest's preferences, like whether they want a smoking or non-smoking room, or whether they prefer beer or mineral water in their rooms.

No matter what you're selling, you can keep records about what each customer has bought in the past. A lot of pizza parlors today have computerized operations so that as soon as the phone rings, a call-capture feature linked to a database prints on a computer screen the customer's name and what they ordered last time. So the salesperson can answer the phone with, "Hello, Mr. Johnson, last time you ordered a large deep dish with pepperoni, would you like that again?" It may freak out your customer the first time this happens, but ultimately it leads to better relationships with them.

Stay in Touch!

I never cease to be amazed at the number of customers who can't recall the name of the salesperson who sold them their car, or house, or boat, or computer. Why? Because the salesperson never stayed in touch! What a waste. The surest way to lose what may have become lifetime customers is to ignore them.

Staying in touch means more than just sending one or two cards. Think about it. A new car may last a customer five years and a home may last them 10 years or more. Even a new computer will probably last a couple of years before being replaced. If all you send is a simple thank-you after the sale, your customer will have no idea who you are when they finally get around to buying again. Staying in touch means establishing a regular system of contacts so that your customer hears from you regularly until the next time they're in the market.

That could mean twice a year or once a month, but it's got to be regular and it's got to be meaningful. You could, for example, send your customer details about the current interest rate situation to keep them abreast of market conditions. This is valuable information and will not only keep your name before the customer, it will establish you in their eyes as an expert in the field.

Whatever you do, don't lose track.

And whatever you do, never forget that a sale is only a gateway to a long-time relationship with your client.

RALPH'S RULE

Study after study has shown that it's cheaper to do business with a repeat customer than it is to go out and find a new one. Learn this lesson. A past customer is your very best prospect.

Do I Use a Soft Sell or a Hard Sell?

Did you ever watch a child in an ice cream shop? He stands before the counter, parents and the sales clerk waiting. The kid will go through the entire list of flavors. In the meantime, other customers are waiting.

Some sales clerks will wait it out, not offering any suggestions, shrugging off the impatient looks of other customers. But sometimes either the sales clerk or the parents begin to make suggestions. "How about this one? You always like this flavor. You've got to make a choice now or you'll lose your turn in line." Pressed this way, the child makes a choice—and generally is happy once he gets the ice cream in hand.

This scenario is a perfect illustration of the difference between a soft sell and a hard sell. Remember, once the child has an ice cream cone—which is what he came into the shop to buy—the dithering back and forth is totally forgotten in the happiness of possession. The only question is, How quickly and easily do we get to that point?

In my industry, I'm known more for my aggressive sales techniques. But, in truth, I use a blend of both hard and soft methods. This strategy must be working. As I've said, I handle some 600 transactions a year. That makes me the most productive Realtor in the United States or Canada.

Admittedly, I may use softer techniques when first building rapport with a customer. I believe I listen to my customers better than almost any other salesperson. You know the old saying that "selling isn't telling"? Burdening your customer with details about the product doesn't work. What works is listening to what really concerns them. It's the old 90/10 rule, that 90 percent of a customer's concerns in a transaction focus on just 10 percent of the actual details. You've got to search out those concerns and address them. I'm careful to ask them how they "feel" about something rather than how they "think" about it. It's gut reactions that give me the information I need to close a deal.

You've got to be sensitive to your clients' needs. And you've got to listen, listen, listen. Most top salespeople like me let their clients do at least 75 percent of the talking. There's an old saying that God gave us two ears and one mouth and if we use them in that proportion we'll come out right.

All this falls under the heading of the soft sell and it's all necessary. But, at the same time, I'll use an aggressive approach, too. Just last month, for example, I went on a presentation to a couple who's in the market to buy a home. I wanted to sell this couple on signing up with us to represent them. I took one of my buyer's agents with me. This other agent is a master of the soft sell. He'll run circles around you to make you feel good about him and about using our company. But when this couple had found a home and it was time for us to make the presentation offer to the seller, they asked me—the more aggressive salesman—to make the offer for them. Why? Because they knew that I'm more focused than anybody on closing the deal. That's what I do best.

In other words, many of our clients want us to use the soft approach early in our relationships, but they definitely want the hard sell when it comes to making things happen.

The phrase "hard sell" has some negative implications, but it needn't. After all, selling is about cutting through all the things that hold up a sale. Buyers are in the market to find what they need. They may be looking for an insurance policy or a minivan or a computer or a dress or any of a thousand other products that we sell. They have all kinds of outside factors trying to gum up the works—their parents or friends offering bad advice, or other buyers and sellers interfering. Selling is about getting to the point that a customer has wanted to reach all along.

To get to that moment of customer satisfaction, you've got to be pretty aggressive on clearing away all the obstacles. I've heard this approach called "hot button closing" or "closing on the objection." If a customer says he wants to bring his wife back to see the product, you may say, "Can we draw up the paperwork now so that all we have to do is put it through when your wife likes this?" Some salespeople find this technique too aggressive, but it has real advantages. It puts the focus squarely on the customer's concern. And it focuses the conversation where it ought to be—on the question of closing.

Many salespeople think they get lucky when they close a deal. But it's their job to close deals. Next time somebody asks you what you do for a living, don't say, "I'm a manufacturer's rep." Say, "I close deals." I get up every morning knowing I'm going to sell a couple of pieces of property that day. Many salespeople in my industry get up hoping they'll sell one property that whole week.

In some ways sales is like a horse race in that little things make a big difference in the outcome. But in other ways it's not like a horse race because in a derby the second and third place finishers still get some prize money. In sales, if you don't finish in first place—if you don't close the deal—you don't get anything.

Let me give you another illustration. Last year, I went on a sales call to convince the seller of a house to let me have the listing. This seller interviewed four different salespeople. He didn't pick me. As is normal in such cases, one of my assistants called to ask why he had chosen another salesperson to list the home. The seller said that "Ralph was too aggressive." We said, "Okay, thanks for that information, we're always trying to make things better." Well, 90 days later, immediately after the listing had expired without the home being sold, that customer called my office. "We want more aggressive," he said and hired me. And I sold the home for him.

If I'm representing a seller like this, I'll try to persuade other salespeople who represent buyers to make an offer on my listing. I'll offer these agents free lunches to show my homes, or I'll offer them easier access at convenient hours, or, since many salespeople in my industry never get the training they need, I'll work with them and their buyers to find a mortgage. I'll show them how to buy my listed home without a down payment. Remember my motivation. I want to make the sale happen!

Soft selling can work, but not to the degree that enthusiasm and energy can multiply your success. I often find that salespeople who use the soft sell aren't as secure, or as well-trained, as more aggressive agents.

Here's a perfect example. Say a buyer is looking at a home, but has some questions about the built-in swimming pool. A soft-sell salesperson might say, "Okay, why don't we call the pool contractor about that and I'll get back to you in a few days." A more aggressive agent like me would reply to the concern this way. "Look, this home may not be on the market by the time we get the information. Why don't we sign the deal right now and include a line that the deal is contingent upon a satisfactory pool inspection?" That way, you make the deal happen right then and there.

Hard selling gets people to make a decision and act. Soft selling is letting the customer control the process. You can literally soft-sell yourself out of a commission.

I believe we need to be sensitive to our customers' needs. We need to build a rapport with them. But the best way to make a customer happy is to help them achieve what they've wanted to do all along. A customer who shops for a new car may hesitate, may show reluctance, may ask a thousand questions. But she's as happy as a kid with an ice cream cone once she drives off the lot in her new car.

To get to that point, you the salesperson have got to cut through the confusion and make it happen.

RALPH'S RULE
Use a soft-sell approach to get in the door and build rapport, but use a hard-sell finish to close the deal.

WEEK 19

My Top 10 Tips for Better Networking

I'm firmly convinced that networking is the heart and soul of every sales career. If you can't network, you shouldn't be in sales. If you can't ask your family, friends, and total strangers for an order, choose another line of work.

Over the years, I've refined my approach to networking. I've kept some things, discarded others. By now, after some 23 years in sales, I've instilled the essence of my experience into my "Top 10 Tips," which are listed below. These are, in my opinion, 10 clear steps to better networking:

1. There's no way around it—you have to network with everyone. You have to network at your kid's school, when you go out to eat, or even when you stop at highway tollbooths. Give your business card to everyone you meet. Ask everyone for an order and/or a referral.

2. When you network, give something to everybody. It can be a business card or your brochure or a flower or even candy. Here's an example. Once upon a time, I parked my car with a valet and handed him my brochure. He ran into the valet booth and showed me a brochure that I had given him during a previous visit. It really got me excited that he had saved my brochure and knew exactly where he kept it. So I looked in my truck and gave him a copy of an inspirational book called *The Platinum Rule* by Art Fettig, which I routinely give to hundreds of people a year. People remember you more often if you hand them something.

3. Don't be afraid of being a little silly or unconventional. When I go to a sports event, I've been known to throw a thousand business cards into the stands. Does even one of those cards ever come back to me as an order? I'll never know. But it sure feels great to know so many people have been exposed to my name.

4. When you attend service club meetings like Rotary, don't always sit with the same five friends. I know you feel more comfortable sitting with familiar faces. But unless you network more widely, you'll be limiting your opportunities to those same five people.

Speaking of service clubs, most of them have rules against giving out your business cards except on specific occasions. They'll fine you a dollar for openly asking for business, because those clubs are supposed to be more social. But I've found that the more dollars I paid, the more business I got. I just hand out my cards all the time at service clubs and cheerfully pay my fines. It's a great form of cheap advertising.

5. Referrals work from the top down, not the bottom up. A boss may pass along the name of a salesman to an employee, but it usually doesn't happen the other way around. So when you network, try to network at the highest level possible. If you're networking car dealers, for example, network the dealership owner before the guy in the body shop. The owner will be in a better position to pass your name along to others.

6. Join or start your own tip club. Tip clubs meet every week and their members try to generate leads for each other. I've joined some lead clubs and started some. You'll get lots of ideas from them and you can network with the other members.

7. Churches can be great places to network. You've got an entire organization of people with like-minded beliefs. Try to put your ad in their weekly newsletter. In fact, offer to pay for producing and mailing it in exchange for free ad space. It's worth every penny!

8. You've got to be seen at all the major events. Big fundraisers, community holiday parties, charitable events. At my level, I go to so many events, it's hard to know which ones bring in new business. But I'm convinced that every time some radio personality interviews me at one of those events, it adds to the bottom line in some way.

9. Have a house account with restaurants where you can sign for meals and get billed monthly. That way, maybe 10 different people at the restaurant see your name on the bill—the waiter, the cashier, the house accountant, secretaries, managers, everyone. And when you pay your bill, include your card or brochure.

10. Get other people to network for you. When I buy clothes, I tell the salespeople that the more successful I am, the more other people will ask me where I buy my clothes, so it's in their own best interests to network on my behalf. And there's a shoe-shine man in Detroit who automatically gives out my brochure every time someone getting a shoe shine mentions buying or selling a house.

RALPH'S RULE

All these tips blend common sense with a little showmanship. But, believe me, they work. I've gotten thousands of transactions to my credit that prove my point. And I firmly believe that if you follow these tips, someday you'll be a top networker and salesperson yourself. Try it!

Use Those Idle Moments

Once I was waiting for a flight connection and the delay stretched longer than we thought. I was getting bored, which always motivates me to make something happen. I bought some cookies. Then I walked around and talked to people, exchanged business cards, and handed out cookies. I wasn't selling anything but name recognition. But I'll bet you that every person I gave a cookie to remembers me and will return my calls.

We find ourselves with idle moments all the time. Salespeople may find themselves in this situation more than most because we're always calling on people and always having to wait. I've tried to add up how much down time I have in my week and, believe me, it's enough to cost me a lot of money if you figure what my time is worth in dollars and cents.

So I always try to find some productive way to use these moments. Maybe I'm on an airplane. Maybe my appointment canceled at the last moment. At these times, I'll make notes in my Franklin planner or make some calls on my cell phone. The important thing is not to let other people's mistakes leave me with a big hole in my day that's costing me money.

Now, I don't mean we're supposed to be workaholics. I tried that in my younger years and, believe me, it's a lot better to have my passion for success under some kind of control. Now I get to spend a lot more time with my family and do many of the things we enjoy together, like bike riding as a family or spending time in our hot tub. I also used to listen to Zig Ziglar tapes before I'd go to sleep, but I learned that I was too pumped up to sleep. I'd have to put on wave sounds at 3 A.M. to calm me down. I love Zig, but maybe you shouldn't listen to him at bedtime!

Now, in fact, I have a new way of getting to sleep. I've put a fire pit in my yard near my hot tub, and sometimes I'll light a fire in it, go up to my bedroom, open the window, and drift to sleep with that wonderful campfire smell relaxing me.

So, anyway, I'm not talking about some sort of workaholic schedule when I say use your time productively. To show you what I mean, let me tell you about Patricia Fripp, a delightful British woman who is a wonderful motivational speaker. Patricia grew up in working-class Britain and became a hairdresser in a barber shop. She always had ambitions to be more than a hairdresser, but she couldn't afford the time or money for a good education. She did it her way. Every time a businessman sat in her chair, she'd quiz him about his company. She gave herself a great education in business and success just by listening. While the other hairdressers were drinking coffee or gossiping about boyfriends, Patricia was getting an education. She jokes today that "all I need to know about life I learned behind the hairdresser's chair!"

That's the kind of productive use of time that I'm talking about. I may work 60 hours a week today (and I used to work 80 to 100 hours) but I'm probably productive only about 40 hours a week. I'm learning how to be more productive, but it's a lifelong process.

So I'd rather have you work 40 hours a week, and fill that time with productive activity, than put in 80 hours and spend half of it spinning your wheels. And when those idle moments pop up, as they always do, find something creative to do with your time. It may help to carry a good planner and review your goals. Or perhaps you can just network as I did in that airport that day. Or maybe you can have a few tasks ready to do when you find yourself stuck. Make sure that they're things you really need to tend to—not just make-work projects. Working on your long-term investment strategy, or reading some success literature, is great.

RALPH'S RULE

Even if you're not meeting with clients, making calls, or tending to paperwork, you can find fun, creative ways to keep your juices flowing.

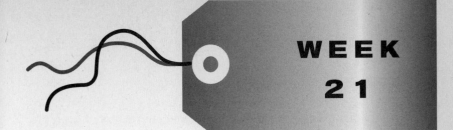

Marketing a Home-Based Business

Stella Borst and Pam Lusczakoski are two women from suburban Detroit who can teach us all about marketing. They run a business called Artistic Accents by Pastel from the basement of Stella's home. Their company sells stencils—a more sophisticated version of the old paint-by-the-number kits we all used as kids. They sell these kits to homeowners, hobby shops, and interior decorators—anyone with an interest in brightening up a home or office.

Now, just because a business is home-based doesn't mean you can neglect marketing. In fact, you probably need to do more of it than ever. A home-based business doesn't have any storefront appeal; no one can window-shop because you don't have any store window for them to walk by. So you've got to get the word out in other ways.

Now, Stella and Pam are as good at this as anybody. They're entirely self-taught, too. "I don't have a degree in marketing," Stella says. "We sit down here and say, 'Who can we pester now?'"

I'll describe a few of their marketing efforts here. I urge you to adopt some or all of these if you operate a home-based business yourself.

Bargain for an Advantage

Stella and Pam were walking through a shopping mall recently when they saw a long blank wall. They quickly decided it would make an ideal display for their stencils. So they struck a bargain with the mall manager. In exchange for decorating the wall with stencils of flowers and trees and birdhouses and picket fences, the mall gave them a small kiosk from which to promote their stencil kits and catalogs. Their decorating efforts at the mall attracted a lot of attention and even made the local newspaper.

In a similar example, the women bargained with a national paint company. They agreed to include the company's brand of paint in the stencil kits in exchange for free promotion by the paint company.

I call these methods zero-based marketing. We use it all the time at my real estate firm. It's a way of getting other people who benefit from your efforts to help pay your marketing costs. For example, mortgage lenders tend to get a lot of referrals from me, so I've asked them to help pay the cost of producing my home advertising flyers. This brings down the cost of producing and mailing these flyers.

Niche Marketing

A lot of home-based firms make the mistake of plunging all their marketing dollars into one big ad in a large general-interest publication. That's a mistake. The ads usually don't work and you've blown your marketing budget.

Stella and Pam spend carefully on ads in a variety of small publications devoted to home decorating. One was the new *1001 Country Decorating Ideas*, a start-up publication that went to exactly the kinds of customers the women wanted to reach. And the two women aren't afraid to ask for extras. In exchange for a $300 ad, the magazine agreed to include a mention of them in an upcoming article.

Seek Feedback Constantly

Every time a customer orders a catalog or a kit, Stella and Pam ask where the customer heard of Artistic Accents. They emphasize whatever draws more customers.

This is a technique that I've used for years. I've tried all kinds of marketing—direct mail, billboards, TV, newspaper ads, the Internet, and much, much more. You've got to give a new marketing technique a few months to work, then evaluate it. If it's making you money, or breaking even, continue it for another few months. If it's losing money, drop it. But when you find something that works, stick with it for as long as it helps you.

Consistency in Marketing

Deciding they'd sell more kits if customers think their stencils are easy to use, Stella and Pam emphasize that even beginners can be stenciling in 20 minutes. Every single piece of marketing underscores this ease of use.

Consistency is so important. Most experts say you shouldn't begin a marketing campaign unless you're confident that you'll feel comfortable with the message five or even 10 years from now.

Set Aside Time Every Week for Marketing

Stella estimates they spend one day a week strictly on thinking up new marketing efforts and implementing them. Less savvy entrepreneurs market only during slack times. But by making it a regular scheduled activity, Stella and Pam increase the odds they'll have fewer and briefer slack periods when those do come.

In short, these two women working in the basement of Stella's home could teach most entrepreneurs a lot about marketing. If you run a home-based business, I strongly urge you to adapt some of their methods to your own company. Good luck!

RALPH'S RULE

Thinking of ways to attract new customers is a 24-hour-a-day, seven-day-a-week activity for a home-business owner. You can never do enough marketing.

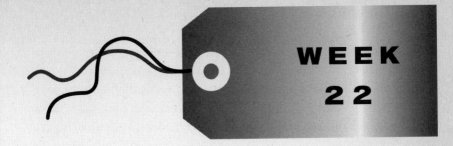

My Five Strategies for Getting the Most out of Technology

Probably half the computer software purchased in America never gets used. It either sits in its shrink-wrapped box on a shelf at home, or maybe it gets loaded into a computer but never called up. Perhaps the buyer uses only a tiny piece of the software program, but never uses its full potential. What a waste.

It's sad because technology, if used properly, can boost your business to new heights of profit and productivity. Certainly that's what I've found at my own company here in Detroit. I never would have been able to reach this pinnacle of success without technology.

Over the years, I've developed some strategies for getting the most out of technology. In this chapter, I'll outline a few of them. Follow them and you'll do more than get the most from your software, voice mail, pagers, faxes, and other technologies. You'll also find yourself steadily rising in the ranks of your profession.

1. The first model introduced may stink, but improved versions follow quickly. This works across a variety of technologies. Consider cellular phones. When I got into my sales career 20 years ago, I was one of the first real estate agents in the country to have a phone in my car. It was clunky and hard to use. The model I carry now in my suit coat pocket is a slim touch-tone model. We even own a few digital communications units that are like walkie-talkies with phones and pagers built in. They're marvelous, with clear-as-a-bell reception. Had I given up on portable phones because the first models were hard to use, I'd never have enjoyed the many improvements that have come along since.

2. Any technology has more than one use, so learn them all. Take, for example, voice mail. Many people see voice mail as just an answering machine—something that will take messages for you. Consequently, many salespeople don't use it correctly. Many salespeople put a greeting on their voice mail and leave it there for five years. Some people let their kids do the greeting at home and the kids have grown and gone off to college and the parents still haven't changed their greeting.

To be a superstar, you need to see voice mail as another proactive tool that will help you succeed. Many top salespeople change their greetings every morning. This lets callers know that you're in the office and interested in their calls. But, more important, the best salespeople exploit all the other features. You can couple your voice mail with a pager, so that a caller can leave you a message that will then page you to let you know it's there. You can also link your voice mail to features like fax machines and call forwarding. Or you can link voice mail with an interactive 800-number system. Callers can browse through a menu to order products, such as my consumer guides to buying a home. On the system I use at my office, callers can ask for information about mortgage loans, and the employee in charge of my mortgage operation will be paged immediately. He can return the call within moments. I can also use the system to weigh the effectiveness of my advertising, because callers key in a code that they've seen in a given ad.

It's all helpful. But none of this would happen if I accepted that only the single, most basic use of voice mail was the only one.

3. Sometimes the best technology purchase is more of the same thing. I now have five fax machines in my office and one in my home. I can't imagine trying to run my business with just a single fax machine. Would you have just one telephone or one computer in your office? Of course not.

By the year 2000, the best salespeople will have not one but three computers on their desks. They might have one tied up to the Internet working all the time, another one making their phone calls and keeping their diary, and another set up doing word processing. I know you're out there reading this thinking you can flip back and forth between screens so you don't need more than one computer. But I believe it depends on how efficient you want to be. Change is accelerating, and I want to stay on top of it.

4. Older technologies sometimes are the best. Consider the humble Dictaphone. I know it's been around a long time, but it has always done wonders for my business. I'm really an idea person. Early in my career, I used to hand-write my ideas, but pretty soon I purchased my first Dictaphone. I'd be driving in my car and think of three things—how to get a listing here, a buyer there, and maybe a promotion we could do—and I'd dictate into my Dictaphone, and my secretary would turn it into a memo. With a Dictaphone, I found I didn't lose track of things. How many times have you had a great idea at night but you didn't write it down, and the next morning it was gone? I'd be nowhere near as successful without this simple but marvelous technology.

By the way, my rule that technology always improves applies here, too. There's a voice-recognition system that I'm looking at that could eliminate the need for my secretary, Betty, to transcribe the tapes at all. The software will do it for us.

5. The best technology is one you use.

Don't be like the people who can't program their VCR, or never unwrap their new software, or leave their pagers in their desk drawers. If you don't use it, why buy it in the first place? But if you put all your technology to the very best use, you'll find your sales and income soaring.

RALPH'S RULE

Learn what your current technology has to offer and use it. Check out the newer technologies regularly. But make sure you will gain from it before buying it. Technology that isn't used to your benefit is useless.

WEEK

23

Using the Internet

By the year 2000, close to one car buyer in four will be using the Internet for the transaction. Already several big Web sites on the Internet are devoted to car shopping. The granddaddy of these, the Edmund's service at edmund.com, gets 50,000 hits a day! It provides competitive prices of cars, which lets consumers comparison shop without ever leaving their homes.

The Internet can be a great tool for a salesperson, but it can also pose a challenge. So powerful is this tool that it empowers consumers. It can provide a shopper with some or all of the information he or she used to get from a salesperson. Richard Everett, director of strategic technologies for Chrysler's sales and marketing operations, told the *Wall Street Journal* recently, "In a very short period of time, the last stupid customer is going to walk through our dealership doors."

What is true of car selling is true across a range of industries. In my business, Realtors used to keep information about home sales a closely guarded secret. Now, more and more information is available publicly to home buyers on the Internet. Not as many consumers take advantage of this source of information in home buying as in car buying, but the numbers are rising.

I believe we all need to get on the Internet and make it work for us. If your customers are using the Net, and if your competitors are using it, too, then you sure as heck ought to be on it yourself. It will keep you competitive with your more aggressive rivals and put you way out in front of lesser salespeople.

First, many of the sales-related Web sites will list your name and product information, sometimes for a fee and sometimes for free. There are so many of these in car buying alone that there's no room to list them here. Try to find the Web sites that deal with your industry and geographic area. Then get in touch with them and find out what you need to do to get listed.

So far, I'm getting only a handful of my 600 transactions from the Internet, maybe two or three a month. I expect that to increase as I develop my system. But I use the Internet in other ways, too, and these are beneficial to me.

For example, the Net allows me to set up a virtual one-stop shop for almost all aspects of the home-buying process. We can sit with a client in my office, browse though all the available listings (shown in full color on a computer screen), apply for and receive approval for a mortgage, and be done in an hour. It's amazing how much the time-consuming process of buying and selling a home can be compressed. What used to take weeks now takes hours or minutes.

I also use my own personal Web site, ralphroberts.com, to market my various motivational and sales-related products, such as publications on how to overcome the most common mistakes in selling. This has been a big help to me and well worth the relatively minor cost of creating a Web site.

In creating your own Web page, remember not to go overboard on the graphics. The jazziest pages often take so long to come up on your screen that consumers move on to something else. Your page ought to boot up within, say, 15 to 30 seconds. Any longer and a surfer may just hit the cancel key.

The other important thing to keep in mind is to get your own domain name. That's the Internet address that stays with you for as long as you want to keep it. Mine is ralphroberts.com. A good Web site designer can help you obtain your own domain name. Don't get fooled by all the bad Web page designers out there. Check them out, do your homework, demand to see samples of their work, and check their references. A good designer can help boost your profits more than you realize.

Finally, as a salesperson you ought to be surfing the Net frequently to check out your competitors' sites and the Web pages devoted to your industry. If you're in one of the sales professions heavily affected by Internet selling, like the car buying industry, this is something you absolutely must do. By the year 2000, the successful salespeople will be on the Internet and everyone else will be out of business.

In fact, there are some market niches where you can sell virtually full-time on the Internet if your product is right. You could devote all your time to Internet sales and marketing and be very successful without ever dealing with customers in person.

I know that there are drawbacks to Internet selling. One of the most common complaints is that Net selling reduces every transaction strictly to price. Every product becomes a commodity and price is the only issue. To some extent that's true, especially in fields like automotive sales. But a savvy salesperson will learn to leverage the raw information available on-line with better service and finer attention to customers' needs.

One final caution: Remember as you spend time on the Internet that you're doing business, not just surfing for the fun of it. Sure, you need time just to surf, but don't get so caught up in the Web and its attractions that you lose sight of why you're on-line in the first place.

RALPH'S RULE

A lot of nonsense has been written about the Internet, but the simple fact that is the Net is transforming our profession. Look at the Internet as an opportunity and a helpful tool rather than as an obstacle.

Reward Yourself Before a Sale, Not After

Probably all salespeople reward themselves for achieving success. So do I. Recently, for example, I bought a barbecue grill. It's a simple yet efficient two-burner stainless steel grill, and I bought a good utensil set to go with it. The grill is anchored to a spot in my yard. I've cooked a couple of dinners on it and I've entertained friends, which I love to do.

By now, perhaps you've guessed that my methods differ from those of most salespeople. Most salespeople reward themselves *after* they close a deal. I reward myself *before*—to motivate myself.

Let me explain. I work hard to give my family a good life. I pay my mortgage, just like most of you. But I always try to create some other reason why I have to keep working. Call it creative tension or whatever you like. Put simply, I like to see the rewards, and I know I work better and harder if I can see the rewards up front.

Sometimes, sure, I'll clip out a picture of what I want and hang it above my desk to motivate me. Other times, though, I'll just buy myself some new suits or the barbecue grill or a hot tub for my yard—before I've got anything special to celebrate. Then I go out and make something happen in my business to pay for it.

If you're starting out in sales, you'll need to be a little careful about this particular advice. I'm sure I could have simply paid for the grill out of cash in my pocket. But I get a special thrill out of buying it and then making something good happen in my business to help me pay for it. And it's a fact that many other top salespeople have developed a habit of rewarding themselves in advance of a sale. My friend Stanley Mills, one of the top real estate salespeople in Tennessee, and Allan Domb, the condominium king of Philadelphia, both follow this practice. For sure, it's not necessarily the clothes or the barbecue grill in themselves that pump me up—it's the excitement they give me. Through a constant flow of gifts to myself and others, I see the tangible fruits of all my hard work. And that serves as a spur to make me work even harder.

By now, I've developed my reward system to a fine degree. For example, I love to use money for free—interest-free, that is. So when I bought my barbecue grill I filled out the store's credit application and got the grill for no money down and no interest for 90 days. Then I paid off the loan in full on the 75th day, because if you go over the 90 days the store will charge interest back to day one.

When I go Christmas shopping in Chicago each year, I often use interest-free credit in this same way. In fact, my goal during the two days we spend shopping in Chicago is to get one new credit card per day. Often the store will give you an extra 10 percent off the price of the item just for applying for the card. So I buy something I want and get a nice discount and not have to pay anything for close to 90 days. I simply use the store's money interest-free. I just love that.

If you think that I must accumulate a lot of credit cards this way, you're correct. I now have many cards—almost all locked away in a vault for safekeeping. And I don't pay an annual fee on any of them. If a card issuer wants to charge me a fee, I cancel the card or just ask the issuer to waive the fee, which they often do.

There are other advantages of my reward system. Once I apply for a card, I get more catalogs delivered at home. I enjoy shopping by catalog, too.

Now, as I said, you have to be careful if you're not familiar with shopping this way. Too many Americans get in trouble with consumer debt. If you're not careful, it could lead to bankruptcy. As my beautiful but more conservative wife, Kathy, puts it: "If we both spent money excessively, we'd be in trouble."

But, with that caution, I have to emphasize that top salespeople like me use this method of rewarding ourselves as a key motivational tool. Most of us are in sales because we like to be able to buy nice things for ourselves and our families. Don't go crazy, and don't buy in advance if you're not comfortable with that. But you need to establish a reward system for yourself. On those down days when nothing seems to be working, thinking ahead to the rewards you've promised yourself will motivate you to get back in there and sell.

RALPH'S RULE

Once you've achieved a certain level of success, you'll find that rewarding yourself on a regular basis motivates you to even greater things.

Six Things to Do When You Lose a Deal

We all lose deals. I hate it. Sometimes we lose when the customer says no, and sometimes we lose after a contract is already signed but the deal just sort of falls apart. We work so hard to make sales happen that I just *hate* it when I lose one. Still, it happens, so we have to be prepared. Here's my checklist of things to do when one of your deals heads south.

1. Save it! That's right, salvage it—somehow. You'd be surprised at how many salespeople just give up on a deal when it runs into snags. They'll consider it lost and move on to the next one. Not me. I believe that 75 percent of "lost" sales can be saved. It takes more work, but a deal saved is a sale made.

Let me give you an example. Recently I was showing a home for sale, and the buyers made an offer contingent upon an inspection. This is standard practice. Well, the inspector found a few inches of standing water in the crawl space in the basement. The buyers wanted to pull out of the deal. But I really wanted to save this sale, so I dug into the situation. I learned from the inspector that the sump pump was defective. The pump wasn't doing its job, and that's why the water had begun to collect. It would cost $250 to fix the pump. I got the seller to pay for the new pump and then I brought my buyers back for another look. They were satisfied that the problem had been fixed. Result: Another sale!

Many of your "lost" deals can be saved in this way. Never give up on a deal until you've done everything in your power to save it.

2. When you do lose a sale, find out why. Okay, so you've hit one of those walls where you just cannot get the sale you've worked on for so long. When this happens, I make a practice of asking the customers why they chose to go in another direction. (Mind, now, I'm not talking about casual shoppers—I'm talking about losing customers who were qualified and ready to buy.) Often, they'll tell me up front. They'll say I was too aggressive, or that they promised a family member they'd use another salesperson, or some other reason. And I always say, "Thanks, that's helpful information, we're always trying to improve."

There are two reasons that I bother to ask. First, the information often is helpful. If I'm coming across as too aggressive too often, maybe I'll tone down my presentation. We all need feedback, and what better feedback than from our customers? But, second, I also use the information to know how to approach those same customers the next time. If, for example, they used another salesperson only because a family member suggested it, that sale has a good chance of not working out, because the customers are choosing a salesperson for the wrong reason. That's good to know when I approach them again.

3. Stay in touch with them. A lot of customers who go elsewhere come to regret it. Maybe the other salesperson your customer chose could not perform as advertised. Quite often, I've found that a customer who gives me an emphatic no is ready to do business with me a month later.

Let me tell you about my friend Jonathan Dwoskin. Jonathan is a top account executive with US Web, one of the largest and best of the Internet consulting firms. I know firsthand the quality of their work because they do my Web site, which you'll find at ralphroberts.com. Not long ago, Jonathan was chasing a deal with a major customer who eventually went with another Web designer. The customer had wanted to hire a firm that could handle its public relations as well as its Internet site. Jonathan said US Web would be happy to bring in a good PR firm as part of its package, but didn't keep that function in-house because US Web wants to focus only on what it does best. Well, the customer went with another Web consultant that promised everything.

"After I lost it, I called her every month," Jonathan says of this customer. "I would ask, 'Are things going okay? Are you being treated like you want?' I continually built that relationship." He never gave up, but always let the customer know in a quiet, professional way that US Web stood ready to serve it.

Well, just before the customer's Web site was to debut—and it was the focus of a huge nationwide marketing campaign that had already been printed—the customer called Jonathan in a panic. The first provider had been unable to deliver. The customer was 10 days shy of launching the campaign and had to meet deadline. Could Jonathan's team take over and finish on time?

Well, they did, and today Jonathan estimates that this one customer will result in a half-million dollars' worth of business over time. US Web got the deal in the end probably for a lot of reasons and not only because Jonathan stayed in touch after he "lost" the first sale. But surely it helped that Jonathan was smart enough to know a deal isn't lost until your competitor has delivered the goods.

4. Thank them for their time. This is simple courtesy, and it's always good business. You can thank them verbally, send them a note, or even send them flowers or a gift. Consider it part of your marketing budget. It will certainly impress those potential customers with your desire.

5. Ask for a referral. A lot of customers may be impressed with your knowledge and professionalism even if they don't sign a contract. They may be willing to refer others to you. Ask!

6. Move on. When you really lose a sale, don't dwell on the failure. Move on! You're a professional, and you know that losses are just part of the game. Your next sale may be just around the corner.

RALPH'S RULE

Failure is part of our business, so you'll need a game plan for dealing with it. Once you have your plan in place, review it frequently. You'll find that losing a deal isn't the terrible setback you once thought it was.

WEEK 26

Where Should You Meet Your Customers?

For many salespeople, the question of where a sales call takes place is a given. You sell clothing in a mall boutique and that's where you meet your customers. Or you sell boats at a marina and you meet buyers in the showroom or on the lot. Or you sell mortgages in a loan office and you talk to customers at your desk.

All well and good. But if, like me, you have some choice of where you meet customers, you ought to give some serious thought to getting this right. This seemingly innocent question actually could make or break the success of your sales call.

Let's start with a given. You always want to discover what your customer *feels* about a transaction, not what he or she *thinks* about it. Buying decisions are made mostly by gut reactions, and you want to learn what hopes, fears, expectations, and desires your customer harbors for whatever you're selling. After many years of close study of this question, I firmly believe some places are more conducive than others to bringing out a customer's true feelings.

For example, when I'm meeting customers in their home, I always try to get them to the kitchen table as quickly as possible. People invite acquaintances or business people to the living room or den, but they invite friends to the kitchen. That's where they're most likely to unwind. That's where they'll reveal their true feelings to you.

Sometimes I have to use a little fancy footwork to get to the kitchen. If I'm trying to get the listing to sell this home and the customer invites me to sit in the living room, I may ask for a glass of water or simply say I want to see their kitchen. I use my gut reactions with each client to judge how easily and how quickly I can accomplish this initial aim of getting to the kitchen table. It doesn't always work, but it always makes my work easier when that's where we have our conversation.

By the way, I think a lot about how to set the stage for my sales call, too. If I'm calling on a husband and wife at their home, which I often do, I like to sit my customers at the corner of the kitchen table, close together, with me at the opposite corner. This way I can see both of them at the same time. I can judge from their eyes and their body language how I'm doing.

You can adapt this principle to almost any setting. If you're meeting customers in a restaurant, try to get them to sit facing you, not the rest of the room. A busy restaurant offers so many distractions that your customers' attention may wander. You want them focused on you alone so you can draw them out about your transaction.

Even if you sell clothes in a mall, you can exercise some choice of setting. You could, for example, approach customers while they're at the clothes rack or stand back in a more reserved posture at the counter. To me, it seems clear that more sales are made at the rack than at the counter, because at the rack you can get truer reactions, as well as demonstrate your expertise about the various lines of clothing. A sales representative who waits at the counter for customers to bring their selections is really just an order taker, not a salesperson in the true sense of the word.

Okay, suppose you make sales calls on companies. Maybe you'll be directed to the purchasing manager's office, or even to the desk of a subordinate. When possible, you ought to suggest that the meeting be held in the executive's private office. Maybe that's obvious, but let's examine why. Even a corporate conference room is not as good as a private office. Conference rooms are remote from the place where the purchasing exec feels comfortable. It's where group decisions are made, often in the negative, as most committee decisions are negative.

Instead, you want to get inside that comfort zone, not in a threatening way, but just so the buyer will let his or her hair down a little and share with you some genuine reactions. At the very least, you may learn why you're not getting the deal at this time. Outside, your customer may have told you that the company just doesn't need your product right now; but perhaps in his office he'll let you know he was disappointed with the servicing last time around. Such honest reactions are crucial to successful selling in the future.

By the way, when you call on a company, try to find out as much as you can about it and its structure. Get the names not only of the purchasing agent and the agent's boss, but the names of the secretaries and the receptionist, too. Take my office, for example. Often another salesperson who's trying to sell me something will call and ask for Ralph, as if he knew me. My receptionist will say I'm not in the office, so the caller will ask, "Is Betty there?" referring to my secretary. Since the caller knows Betty's name, our receptionist will put the call through to her. Maybe we won't want to buy anything that day, but at least the caller knows enough to get a step closer to the decision maker in the office.

In the same way, the more you know about how a company works, the better the odds you'll be able to complete your sales call successfully.

RALPH'S RULE

Sales success is a matter of details. I can think of no situation where you couldn't improve the odds in your favor by a little artful stage setting. Give this problem some thought, and I bet you see results.

Staying Put

High turnover among staff is one of the things that kills any business, from fast food to the biggest corporations. I believe it's especially damaging to sales organizations. Believe me, I've tried it both ways—jumping from job to job, and then staying put for a decade with one firm—and I know that staying put definitely is better.

I've observed that most salespeople jump from company to company hoping for a better commission split or a nicer boss or better hours. I did that myself when I was younger. I changed real estate firms seven or eight times, always hoping for a better arrangement, before I finally opened my own company about 10 years ago. I realize now how silly it was for me to think all that moving from company to company would do me any good.

It's clear to me that there is no perfect company or any ideal marketplace. You make money by digging deep where you are right now and making it happen here and now. The only thing that switching from firm to firm accomplishes is to waste your time and resources.

Recently, I read in the *Wall Street Journal* how an auto deal consultant named Mark Rikess has studied how a high turnover rate in the sales staff can damage a auto dealership's bottom line. Rikess estimates that auto dealerships with high staff turnover must hire one supervisor for every 2.3 salespeople. Because of inexperience, the novice car salesperson handles just seven transactions a month. And each transaction may take four hours to complete on average.

In contrast, an experienced staff requires much less supervision. Veteran auto salespeople can double the number of transactions per month (and the great auto salespeople may do 30 or more transactions a month—a sale a day). Veterans also need only one hour per deal instead of four. Quite a savings for the dealership!

Even for the individual salesperson, savings are possible if you stay put. Every time I switched real estate firms, I had to buy new business cards and let my client base know where I was. I had to create new stationery. I had to develop new marketing materials. Each time, I lost a lot of momentum. And, of course, I had to learn a whole new system with each new company.

Was it worth it? No, it wasn't. In hindsight I think it's clear all those moves cost me more money than they made me.

Sometimes you'll have a serious disagreement with your boss. You may have different goals for yourself than your boss does. If these disagreements are serious enough, then, yes, perhaps you ought to make a move. But don't give in to that temptation to move every time you run into a routine disappointment at the office. Instead, I'd take some of that energy and put it into making things better where you are.

Perhaps you can negotiate a different commission split, or get your boss to pay for new marketing materials for you. Maybe your company will pay to get you some additional training or to send you to your industry's annual convention. Any of these steps would make you a more professional salesperson, and probably a happier person. It would ease the disappointment that was making you think of moving on.

Try it next time you're tempted to move. What can you lose? If it doesn't work, you can always go somewhere else. But you may find that your working conditions and/or pay improve, just for the asking.

RALPH'S RULE

The most successful salespeople are the ones who make things happen where they are, not the ones who jump ship to new companies every year, hoping to find happiness somewhere else.

How to Ask and Answer Questions

One of the themes of this book is that you've got to treat your customers with respect. Don't lie to them, don't try to manipulate them, give them your very best advice and work for a long-term relationship, not for a short-term sale. That's the best advice I can give you.

At the same time, I don't want you to carelessly talk yourself out of a sale through verbal mistakes. There are good ways and bad ways to negotiate a deal. If a transaction is not in the customers' best interest, don't try to force it on them. But when a deal is exactly what they want and need, you still need to be careful not to upset the chemistry that has gotten your customers to the brink of saying yes.

I always practice a form of sales talk that emphasizes listening on my part and asking lots of questions. I never ask questions that a customer can answer with a simple yes or no. One-word answers kill the conversation. For another thing, they don't tell me anything. As a salesperson, I've got to uncover my customer's emotional reactions to this pending sale. So my first rule of sales talk is this:

Ask Questions That Require Some Explanation from Your Customer

For example, I never ask home sellers what price they want to list their house for.

That would get a reply like "$160,000." Instead, I'll ask what factors go into the customers' thinking about the price. They may tell me their friends down the street sold their house for that much. And now I understand more about their expectations and what I have to do to bring them around to a realistic price.

In the same way, I avoid giving simple, direct answers to many questions that customers ask me. And for the same reasons, too. I don't want to kill the conversation; rather, I'm looking for ways to draw out my customers so I can understand their feelings. For example, if the customers ask me what I think of a price of $175,000, instead of saying it's too high or too low for their house, I may say something like, "Tell me why that price appeals to you." The goal is to get the customer talking about the concerns that lie behind their questions. Once you know those concerns, you're in a much better position to counsel your client.

So my next rule for sales talk is simple.

Try to Answer a Question with a Question of Your Own

You've also got to be careful not to unsell your product. If the customers ask me how big a home lot is, if I answer directly by saying "150 by 80," I may scare them off for some reason. Maybe they think that lot size is too big or too small. So I'll ask, "How big do you want it?" And they may say something like, "Not too big because I don't want to have to mow the lawn." And then I can say, "That's great because this lot is average for its neighborhood and not too big."

In the same way, if a caller asks how many bedrooms does this home have, the answer isn't three or four. The correct answer is, "How many bedrooms do you want?" If they say three, I can say, "Great, this home has three bedrooms and a den." Or if they said four, I might reply, "Great, this is a four-bedroom home but the current owners are using one of the rooms for a den."

Even if your product isn't directly what the customer wants, you can still answer questions by pointing out the advantages of what you're selling. Don't push it so far that you annoy the customer, but you need to guard against losing a deal that's good for your customer through a careless answer.

Another rule is this:

Break Down Bad News into Terms That Are Easier to Accept

For example, suppose the customers tell me that a home price is $10,000 more than they think they can afford. Instead of saying the deal's over, I'll ask them what they think that $10,000 means in terms of a monthly payment. Maybe they have some exaggerated idea of what their monthly obligations would be. And I'll say, "What if I can show you that extra $10,000 means only $2 a day more in your payments? Or $60 a month?" Or something like that. I'll keep working with them to break down this scary-sounding number to something they can more easily understand.

Sometimes their fears or emotional reactions are based on erroneous thinking. And sometimes these fears can put them out of a sale that really could be good for them. It's our job as salespeople to make sure that doesn't happen. I don't want you to force any deals that are bad for your clients; but also I don't want you to let a good transaction get away simply because you asked or answered a question in a careless way.

RALPH'S RULE

Talking to a customer is an art form. It involves getting the customers to reveal what they really feel about your product or service. If you can guide the conversation to that point, you'll find both you and your customers are happier.

Telephone Sales

Recently my wife, Kathy, had a special birthday, and I wanted to buy her the car of her dreams—a red convertible Corvette. Since I didn't have time to go from showroom to showroom, I started making calls from my office each day. And every Corvette sales-man I talked to refused to quote me a price over the phone. It was maddening! One would say, "We can't give you that over the phone, you'll have to come in," and I would say, "You know what? That's what the last salesperson who's not going to sell me a car today told me." Finally, I found a salesperson who said he had the car I wanted. He quoted me a price and said he'd hold it for me. "Great," I told him, "I'll be there in two hours." And in two hours when I arrived this guy told me that another customer had put down a deposit on that car and it was no longer available. I was steamed!

So far, this little story has been about how *not* to do telephone sales. Rude, evasive, unhelpful telephone calls don't do anybody any good—not the salesperson and not the customer. Yet telephone sales are a necessary part of almost any sales career today. You may believe, as I do, that face-to-face selling at a customer's kitchen table is better than selling by phone; face-to-face selling gives us a better feel for a customer's emotional reactions than telephone sales do. But let's face reality. In this day of national and international accounts and high-volume business, selling by phone is a must.

But, as my story of Corvette shopping proves, there are right ways and wrong ways to do it. All those initial salespeople just turned me off the idea of working with them. Do you know what the commission is on an $50,000 car? Think of how much money those salespeople lost by not being helpful over the phone.

Basically, the right way to do telephone sales remains the same as in face-to-face selling. You treat your customers with respect. You don't lie to them. You don't make promises you can't deliver, like that auto salesman I just told you about.

But let me finish my story. I returned to my office, and over the next couple of weeks I continued to search by phone for the right car. And finally I found a man named Lew Tuller in a dealership in Dearborn, Michigan. I'm convinced now that Lew is the best Corvette salesperson in the country. I told Lew what had occurred and he took over and made everything happen—quoted me the price, found the car, faxed me the credit application, everything. I couldn't have been happier!

What made the difference? Lew treated my telephone contact as a potential sale to be made right there on the phone—not as a tactic to get me into the showroom. He treated me like an intelligent buyer. He made himself a fan for life.

Here, then, are my rules for successful telephone sales:

Make a Lot of Calls

Years ago I met a Realtor named Allan Domb, the condominium king of Philadelphia, who makes 100 phone calls a day. I didn't think it was possible to make that many. So I went to Philly for a day to shadow Allan—just to watch him work. And through speed-dialing and multiple phones and two secretaries to help him, Allan does indeed make his 100 calls a day. I was so impressed that I made that my own goal. I now have two telephones on my desk. If I'm on hold waiting for one call to go through, I'll often pick up the other and make a second call. Sometimes I have to juggle the receivers a bit, but it usually works out fine.

From this experience I've uncovered a simple yet dynamic truth—the more calls you make, the more money you'll earn. It's a numbers game. The more contacts you make, the better chances you have of uncovering that customer who was just waiting for your call. Don't be afraid to keep calling back at regular intervals, either. Jim Good, one of America's best trainers of telemarketers, tells of how a bottled water salesman visits his office every month or so. Jim has always turned him down. But eventually, Jim says, he's probably going to feel like buying bottled water just when that salesperson stops by. Telephone sales is the same thing. Keep calling and eventually someone will be in a mood to buy.

I tell my sales staff to make 25 phone calls a day in addition to all their other work. I can't set that as a goal for them unless I'm willing to go beyond that to set an example. And that's what I try to do with my 100 calls a day. I don't always reach that goal, but I always make dozens of calls.

So that's my first rule. Make a lot of calls. The more you make, the richer you'll be.

No Scripts

Back in the 1970s, when I was starting out in sales, I read a lot of the sales books that were popular then. Most of these books gave us specific things to say to customers in any situation. These were scripts to follow. And I'd call a customer and deliver one of these scripted lines and the customer would say, "Those are the exact same words that the other salesman said to me yesterday." People can tell when you're not sincere. They can tell when you're just giving them a line.

So stay away from canned remarks. You've got to get some of your own personality into your relationships, whether on the phone or in person.

The "Mirroring" Technique

When you're on the phone, you don't have your customer's body language to read, so you have to find some other way to judge the situation. I find that it helps to mirror the words or conversational style of my customers. We have such a short time to build rapport that you need something to separate you from the pack. On the phone you may have one minute or less to get something going. So, if my customer is loud and brash, I'll try to be the same. If the client talks at a slower pace, I'll slow down, too. If my customer is a little tentative, or brisk and self-assured, I'll try to play that back to the customer.

Mirroring may sound like a gimmick, but in fact it's a good way to get on the customer's wavelength so you can move on to the more important parts of the call.

Have Something to Say When You Call

Most of your calls may be just a way to stay in touch, but you still ought to have something to say. For example, if I lose a deal to another salesperson, I'll call the customer in a few weeks and ask how the deal is working out. Is she happy with her salesperson? Is the level of customer service what she expected?

Or say I'd sold a home to a family a few years ago. I may call them to let them know that interest rates have come down quite a bit since they purchased their house. Would they like to consider refinancing? This kind of call accomplishes two things. First, since I have my own mortgage company, it may find me a new customer for that. But, second, it also establishes me as a thoughtful expert in the eyes of my customers. They may not want to refinance just then, but chances are when they do need to, they'll remember me.

So try to have something useful to offer when you call. It will lessen the likelihood of somebody just hanging up on you.

By the way, telephone sales are a particularly good way to stay in touch after you've made an initial face-to-face contact. A customer whom you see in person only once a year will forget all about you unless you call them several times in between to maintain the relationship.

Smile!

Customers can tell whether you have enthusiasm for them and their problems. So put a smile into your voice. Don't fake it—the customer can detect that. But try to work up some honest enthusiasm for your calls.

Believe it or not, I keep a mirror in front of my telephone to let me know if I'm smiling. Crazy? I don't think so. Not when it helps me sell 600 homes a year!

RALPH'S RULE
Like any sales tool, the telephone is only as helpful as we make it. Done correctly, telephone sales can boost your productivity to heights you never imagined.

A Sale a Day

In my industry, the average salesperson does a transaction about once a month. By my early 30s, I was famous for doing a sale a day. As I write today, my office systems are humming along so well that we average two transactions per day. Working at that pace may sound impossible to you if you're starting out, but there's no reason you can't tremendously increase your production if you follow a few simple rules every single day.

First, you must do the hardest thing on your agenda first thing. Most salespeople do the easy stuff first. They answer their voice mail and they return phone calls and they handle a lot of the routine chores around the office. They keep putting off the hardest task until later in the day, by which time it's looming as an all but impossible thing to get done. And the next day it's even harder. I've learned to do the hardest thing first so that everything after that becomes easier.

After the hardest thing, you've got to do the most dollar-productive task. Elsewhere in this book I give you some ways to determine what that is. For now, just remember that some jobs will pay you a lot more than others, and it's up to you to concentrate on the most important ones.

Okay, we've got you started. You're motivated, smart, and eager for success. But you're getting overwhelmed with the rush of everyday demands. Everybody wants a piece of your time—your boss, your customers, other salespeople. We may work 100 hours a week but we're probably productive only half that time because we waste so much time on unimportant stuff. How do you turn that around? How do you choose the activities that really matter?

I've developed a simple checklist of things I do every single day. These are activities that produce new sales. If I do these things, I'll get more transactions. If I don't do these, I won't. It's as simple as that.

If, for example, I say you should make 25 new contacts each day, and you work six days a week, that's 150 new contacts a week. If you work 50 weeks a year, that's 7,500 new contacts each year. Let's say you need 100 new contacts to create one transaction. That would mean 75 new transactions a year. Seventy-five transactions in my business would put any Realtor at the top of the market.

This kind of success is there for you if you're willing to follow my checklist.

Plan Your Day

I am a tremendous believer in the value of taking 15 minutes each morning to plan my day. I use a Franklin planner and its well-known system of prioritizing daily tasks. I write down what's really important to me, including personal matters like attending my children's school activities. I rank the major items in order of importance. Then I do them and check off each as it gets done. This is a tremendously powerful tool for achieving concrete goals. Planning forces me to write down my goals for the day and attend to them before I get lost in the chaos of a typical day.

I'm reminded of a story about Henry Ford. A man once approached Ford and offered him the secret of success if Ford would give him $10,000. Ford agreed. So the man gave Ford an envelope. Inside was a letter with these simple instructions. "1. Write down everything you need to do today. 2. Do them." Ford chuckled and paid up, acknowledging the correctness of the advice.

Make Sure You Have Plenty of Business Cards to Hand Out to Everyone You Meet

Elsewhere in this book, I talk extensively about the importance of personal marketing. I spend more than $100,000 a year on marketing alone. Our business grosses more than $7 million, so as a percentage it's not too high, but that's still a big number. It covers mailings and billboards and all kinds of things.

But one of the simplest and best kinds of marketing you can do is just carry lots of business cards and give them out to everybody. Don't worry if somebody throws one away. Someone may come along and pick it up and call you. My business cards all have my photograph on them. When I give them to strangers, I've created another potential customer because now someone else knows who I am and what I do. I even give out cards while I'm traveling on out-of-town trips. It not only creates new customers, but it energizes me.

Make Contact with All Your "A" Prospects

An "A" prospect is one that could easily be turned into a sale with just a little more work. This may be one of your regular customers who orders something from you every week or month. Or it could be a new customer who has prequalified himself by calling your office ready to buy. Whoever they are, these are the prospects to work first. No matter what you sell, from boats to cars to houses to cosmetics, there are always people on the verge of buying. As you get established you'll meet more and more of these "A" prospects. It's up to you to stay with them until they're ready to buy.

Turn Two "B" Prospects into "A" Prospects

A "B" prospect is maybe a past customer who isn't looking to buy right now or perhaps a casual looker who told you he may be in the market to buy in a few months. You've had these people on your contact list for a while but haven't talked to them in some time. Each day, take two such people and make something happen with them. In my business, for example, I may call a customer I sold a home to last year and suggest it may be time to refinance the mortgage. Since I have my own mortgage company now, this is another source of profit for me. Or I may call someone who wasn't ready to buy or sell a few months ago and let him know that market conditions have become more favorable for him.

The key is to make something happen. The more "B" prospects you turn into "A" prospects, the more transactions you'll have at the end of each year.

Make 25 New Contacts

After years of working at it, I've settled on 25 new contacts a day as a reasonable number for each salesperson. You may not make it every day, but you've got to try. Remember, in many ways sales is a numbers game. The more people you ask for a sale, the more sales you'll get. Telemarketers know this. They may get a yes only one time in 500, but if they make their 500 calls they know they'll have one sale.

Even if you're busy and making money, don't neglect these calls. Someday your current boom will slow. If you haven't been making your daily calls, you'll have no new business to carry you through this valley.

Make One Referral to Someone Else on the Team

Referrals are critical for our success. It's important to give them as well as get them. Even for a salesperson who likes to work alone, success can become a matter of team effort. In my industry, I used to refer home buyers to mortgage lenders and real estate lawyers and title companies. In exchange, they would refer customers to me. In the past few years, I've made this process internal since I now have my own title company and mortgage firm. The salespeople within my companies are constantly looking for ways to team up and refer business to one another. So, whether you're working with people from your own organization or from outside it, the underlying concept remains the same. If you give something good away, something good will come back to you.

Ask for Referrals from 10 Other People

You can ask for referrals from everybody—other salespeople, past customers, friends, family, strangers. I include a referral form with every sales presentation I make. I don't even wait to close one deal before I'm asking for my customer to refer me to somebody else. Remember, people tend to refer other people like themselves, so one customer may know somebody else who is also in the market for your product. Referrals are like past customers in that they come prequalified. They're always better than simple cold calls.

Make Sure You're on Track to Make Regular Contact with Your Sphere of Influence

A sphere of influence refers to those 200 people that everyone knows—friends, family, associates, acquaintances. We all have them. If you start adding up yours, you'll find you know at least 200 people. This sphere of influence should form the core of your marketing efforts. Let everyone know what you do. It may take you a month to get through the list, but at least every month you ought to send a postcard or make some other contact with your sphere. If you do, the odds will increase astronomically that they'll refer more new business to you.

RALPH'S RULE

Success isn't all that complicated. It's a matter of planning your work and working your plan. If you do what you're supposed to do every single day, by the end of the year you'll be amazed by your new success.

Don't Let a Week
Go By . . .

A week is a reasonable amount of time in which to assess your progress. Daily assessments may not do you much good, given how busy you'll get and how overwhelmed you'll be by everyday events. In fact, some planning experts recommend weekly planning rather than daily planning for this very reason. By the end of each week, you ought to be able to judge whether you're on track and making progress.

Each week, I make sure I do certain things. These are tasks that have become second nature to me by now. I consider them essential for my success. In an earlier chapter I gave you a daily checklist for success, but consider this your weekly checklist—things to make sure you do every single week.

Your Weekly Checklist

1. Plan and review. On Sunday night or Monday morning, review what's left over from the previous week and what you want to accomplish this week. Again, this may sound simple, but you'd be amazed at the number of salespeople who go to work Monday morning and just start putting out fires, rather than working according to any plan.

2. Set goals for yourself for the week. Here are the kinds of goals I'm talking about. "This week I'm going to call at least 100 people. This week I'm going to talk to my 10 best customers. This week I'm going to ask 50 people for referrals." Once you've set a goal, break it down to what you have to do each day to reach it. Asking 50 people for referrals means asking just 10 people a day, and surely you must talk to 10 people each business day.

3. Set aside a few hours each week to review your marketing and promotional campaign. Never skip this all-important step. Every salesperson should constantly be asking how he or she can get the word out to potential customers. Spend at least a couple of hours per week devising some new marketing strategy, even if it's as simple as calling local newspaper editors to ask for coverage or handing out your business card at the supermarket. Once you decide what to do, go out and get it done.

4. Do at least a thumbnail review of your financial situation— your goals, your investments, your debts. Determine each week whether you're making progress or whether some adjustment may be necessary. A major review of your financial situation can take place monthly and yearly, but on a weekly basis you ought to do a back-of-the-envelope calculation where you are for the year.

5. Clear up any administrative problems at your office. These back office chores may slip from day to day, but letting them slip week to week tends to lead to chaos in the end.

6. Have a date with your spouse and a day off with your family. If you're single, devote a day off to your friends. Use this time to develop a hobby like cooking or golf or boating. But get away from the office at least once a week. It will not only help nurture your marriage and your friendships but the recovery time you give yourself will also make you that much more productive on your job. Many 100-hour-a-week salespeople don't believe it, but many of these workaholics find they actually make more money if they cut back to 60 hours or so.

RALPH'S RULE

Checklists are a simple way of focusing on what's important. They'll help you plan your week and they'll assist your review of the week just finished. Over time, a good weekly checklist will make you much more efficient and productive.

Your Monthly Checklist

By the end of each month it ought to be fairly obvious to you whether your plan is working. You'll either be on target for your yearly goals or you should be able to figure out why. It's important that you take time every month to do this kind of review. Success is a matter of little steps that add up to a big journey. A trend that you may not be able to see on a daily or weekly basis may become clearer looked at month to month.

To assist you in this process, I've developed a monthly checklist. These items are essential for any entrepreneurial salesperson, no matter what your field. As long as you're out there in the trenches every day, meeting customers, making calls, you ought to find a way to work the following items into your monthly calendar.

Your Monthly Checklist

1. Contact your entire sphere of influence. Your sphere consists of the 200 to 250 people who make up your family, friends, and circle of acquaintances. Call or send them a note or perhaps a new brochure you've developed. Let them know what you're doing and how much you have to offer. Of course, you can't squeeze this contact work into a single day. It has to be something you schedule and work at a little every day. But over the course of a month, you should be staying in touch with everybody.

2. Renew the cycle of your promotional mailings. Even if you only mail to your client base every other month, you can schedule it so you do half your mailings one month and the other half during the following month. But don't let 30 days go by without having sent out some promotional material to your marketplace.

3. Evaluate your progress toward your financial goals for the year. By the end of each month it ought to be clear whether you're on track. If so, continue to work your plan. If not, reassess and possibly make some changes. Talk to friends and advisers if you need help.

4. Attend at least one networking session. This can be a social/business group like the Chamber of Commerce or one of the numerous tip clubs across the nation. Make friends, make connections. Go more often if possible; many top salespeople attend these networking sessions once a week or more often. But at a minimum I think you need to go to one at least once every month.

5. Contact your local media at least once. Getting covered in the media is the sort of free advertising that we love but can't often get. But if you develop a goal to be the local "expert" in a given field and work diligently to bring yourself to the attention of editors, eventually you'll succeed. You may have to work this plan for a long while before editors and reporters start calling you regularly, but contacting them by phone or mail on a monthly basis is a great way to begin.

6. Assess your need for help in the office. If your work is slipping behind schedule and things are falling through the cracks, chances are you need to hire your first—or your next—assistant. You may not be able to tell whether daily and weekly headaches are signs you need help or are just routine problems. But looked at monthly, the trend ought to become clear. Elsewhere in this book and in *Walk Like a Giant, Sell Like a Madman* I talk about how to hire and train assistants. On a monthly basis you ought to be formally considering the idea.

7. Talk to your advisory group about your goals. Your advisory group can be as simple and informal as your best friends from school or a mentor who helped tutor you in your first job. But you ought to be reviewing and assessing your progress regularly with people you trust.

8. Take at least one weekend off each month to spend with your family and friends. Get out of town if possible. Go to the beach or to a weekend cottage somewhere. I understand you may have to make calls occasionally from your cell phone, but don't overdo it. You really do need some down time at least once a month. And you need to take time for your family's sake. If you feel overwhelmed by work demands, then schedule this time off the same way you schedule business meetings.

RALPH'S RULE

If daily and weekly checklists are designed to help us get work done, a monthly checklist is more to help us review and chart progress. Such reviews are essential to meeting your longer-term goals.

Do the Obvious

Much of the advice in this book deals with doing extraordinary things. I'll show you how to work smarter and harder than your competition. I'll help you to build a better marketing plan and to supercharge the work of your assistants. Getting to the top requires a super effort, and I'll show you just how to achieve that.

Getting to the top requires that you also do the obvious. Things like staying in touch with your past clients. Rewarding your assistants for their extra effort. Networking and self-promotion. I will devote this chapter to reminding you not to neglect the obvious.

Let me tell you about a friend of mine. John Gagliano is a lot like me. He was born and raised in a working-class neighborhood. He went into business right after high school, as I did. And he's a self-made man and a major financial success, also like me.

John had a dream when he was a younger man. He wanted to run the world's best chain of auto collision repair shops. John loved cars and loved tinkering, and the thought of getting his hands on cars that need work made him really happy.

Today, John is president of Collex Collision Experts, a growing chain of auto repair shops. John has about a dozen shops today; his mission statement calls for him to have Collex shops all over the Midwest. He'll do it, too. I know enough about John's motivation and his style to feel confident that he'll reach his dream.

Anyway, John came to one of my Monday sales seminars to talk about his methods. He talked about some of the little extras he did to set his business apart from his competitors—like giving free car loaners to customers while their vehicles were being repaired. These loan cars are painted white and have a huge Collex logo on the side, effectively turning them into moving billboards for his firm.

John said something else that had a powerful effect on me. It struck me as a powerful illustration of doing the obvious.

Before John opens a new Collex shop, he first makes a careful study of available sites. One rule of thumb he always follows in selecting potential sites is for them to be close to local high schools. High school kids drive a lot of beat-up cars and they have a lot of accidents. Their cars quite often wind up in the shop. When that happens, John is there for them.

This struck me as so simple yet brilliant. Of course! Put your collision shops near the people who'll use them the most. That strategy may not sound extraordinarily clever to you, but it doesn't have to be. John just does the obvious, and it's paying off for him in spades.

There are plenty of obvious things you should be doing that many salespeople neglect. You ought to be networking, creating your own marketing materials, and going to seminars and conventions to learn more about your industry. These things are obvious, but you'd be surprised at all the millions of salespeople out there who don't even bother taking the time or effort.

Let me give you another example. About 20 years ago, when I was a young man, and I was running the Overtime Saloon that I told you about earlier, I was also building houses on the side. (I still do, but of course today I have a whole crew to handle all the management and construction work for me.) Anyway, just recently I got a call from a man who had bought one of my houses 20 years ago. He's lived in the same home all these years. He called me because his shower door in the bathroom broke and he wanted to ask where he could buy the fittings to repair it.

Well, I didn't know, because I didn't keep the records from that long ago. But you can be sure that I sent somebody over to look at his door and find the fittings for him. In fact, I'm thinking of buying him the door and installing it for free, just for the promotional value and to thank him for remembering me.

But here's the key: Why do you think he called me after all these years? Why didn't he just go to Home Depot or the local hardware store? Here's why: Every month for 20 years that man got something from me in the mail. It may have been a Christmas card, or a reprint of some article about me, or just a how-are-you-doing letter. But maintaining contacts with my past customers has become as natural to me as breathing. Long ago, I learned that your best customers are the ones you've sold something to. All great salespeople in any field—cars, insurance, real estate, department stores—know that past customers and referrals can make up at least half of your sales, and sometimes a lot higher.

So staying in touch with this man was another example of doing the obvious. And when he decides one day to sell his house, which Realtor do you think he's going to call? You got it. And the commission I'll earn from that sale will more than pay back the tiny cost of sending him a monthly mailing all these years or fixing his shower door!

RALPH'S RULE

You need to be as creative as you can in looking for new business. But you've got to do all the day-to-day things, too. Success is built on a foundation of little things done well. Don't neglect the obvious!

Dealing with Disappointment

You might think that superstar salespeople like Stephen J. Hopson, the deaf stockbroker we met earlier, would be immune to the everyday disappointments most salespeople face. That, of course, isn't true. Stephen and I and all other top producers face adversity all the time. Superstars may recover faster from these crushing blows, but we still feel them. We're still human, after all!

To illustrate, I'll let Stephen tell you about some of his biggest disappointments during his days with Merrill Lynch.

"Here was an investment account I really wanted," Stephen says. "It was a $6 million account with a school for the deaf. I had investment specialists flown in for a meeting with the school officials. I thought it was a done deal but it fell apart weeks after that. I had no inkling it was to fall apart but later found out the school was undergoing a severe budgeting crisis with the State of New York. Unfortunately, it was too late to save the deal. In fact, I don't think I would have been able to save it regardless of what I tried to do.

"Here's another one. I had another investment specialist come with me to a meeting with a wealthy businesswoman who owned a toy manufacturer. She had several investment accounts sprawled all over the place (I often advised my clients to consolidate their investments). This was our advice for her. She liked our presentation and once again, I thought it was a done deal. A few months later her company went under and declared bankruptcy.

"Another time I was interviewed for CNN in 1995. The interview was shown all over the world continually for one full weekend. I thought this would generate thousands of calls. It did not ... but I did get one call from a woman in Seattle who claimed to be super wealthy. I wined and dined her to no end. Eventually I found out she was a fraud. What a disappointment! I couldn't 'save' that one, either!"

I could give you my own list of horror stories like Stephen's, and so could every other top producer. But what makes us different from most salespeople is how we handle such disappointments. We've set up systems to keep on us track so that if one deal falls through, another one already is in place to fall back on. We also use motivational techniques like visualizing our success to keep us charged up for the next deal.

Stephen, for example, keeps what he calls his "One- to Ten-Year Plan." It's a goal booklet that is broken down into four sections. (1) Spiritual/Personal Development; (2) Contributions to Society; (3) Adventures/Toys; and (4) Income/Rewards. Examples of specific goals include happiness, joy, a BMW, and major awards for public speaking, to name a few. Working with his goal book recharges his energies and soon he's back in business.

If all you have going for you is one big deal, sure you'll feel crushed when it falls apart. But if you've got your systems of marketing and self-promotion and client follow-up all in place, you'll find you don't "need" any one given deal. Even the biggest could fall through and you'll still find you can have a good month or quarter or year.

Yes, you'll feel keen disappointment and you'll regret the lost time, but you'll come to understand that these moments are just bumps on the road to your ultimate success.

RALPH'S RULE

Being a success doesn't mean never feeling the sting of failure. It means moving on in the right direction in the face of disappointment.

Exceed Your Customer's Expectations

What's the difference between Disney World and an ordinary amusement park? Expectations. The actual rides and attractions may not be very much different. But Disney consistently exceeds its visitors' idea of what to expect from a resort. Disney provides a total family entertainment environment, not just a ride here and a ride there. It's Disney's ability to go beyond what vacationers expect that has made Disney World one of the most famous vacation destinations.

We can learn from Disney World's experience. Achieving a successful sale is largely a matter of exceeding customer expectations. Notice I don't say that closing a transaction by itself is enough to qualify a deal as successful. It's not. Remember, we're trying to set up long-term relationships with customers, not tag them for one-time commissions. Your customers of today will be back only if you exceeded what they expected.

How to do that? Well, over time you'll get a better feel for your marketplace and for what customers expect. But until you can go merely by instinct, here are a few rules I've found helpful for exceeding expectations.

Ask!

A salesperson should be asking questions all the time. For example, you'll want to know who's going to be using the product and under what conditions. If you work in a boating store and you're selling life jackets to an adult, the first thing you'll have to ask is who's going to wear it—an adult or a child. But you'll also want to ask what kind of boating will be involved. A life jacket that's adequate for a child splashing around in a river or on a canoe trip won't be adequate for someone who goes on serious offshore boating trips. Ask until you get all the information you need to serve your customer.

Remember, the word "ask" consists of three letters: *A* is for "ask"; *S* is for ask "simply" rather than in complicated or overly clever ways; and *K* is for "keep on asking."

Try to Uncover Soft Expectations

Customers usually have both obvious expectations about a product or service and hidden, or soft, expectations. A car buyer may tell the salesperson she expects to pay $20,000 and get a car with air conditioning and antilock brakes. But the unspoken demand may have more to do with expectations of long-term reliability. Many car buyers expect not to have any serious trouble with a new car for five years at a minimum. A salesperson who's used to selling on points like style and engine power may be mystified when a customer leaves for another dealership. But product reliability is one of those softer expectations that becomes crucial to making a connection with your customer.

Often a customer isn't even aware of these softer expectations. Suppose you sell photocopy machines to small businesses. The customer may tell you he needs a machine that can collate and staple and do both color and black and white; but, again, there may be expectations that are even more important. Simplicity may be a concern; he may want everyone in his office to be able to use the machine so he doesn't have to dedicate a separate employee to copying duties. Or he may expect the seller to provide free training and on-site same-day service in case of a breakdown. These are the softer expectations that often do not come out in typical sales calls. But these are the ones that will make or break the long-term relationship.

Follow Up

You should always call your customers shortly after they've taken delivery. Even though product quality has improved over the years, some bad products still get shipped. It's up to us to make sure our customers are happy with what we've sold them. Ask if it's working okay, if the delivery staff was helpful, and if there's anything else we can do. If there's even a hint of trouble, you've got some more work to do trying to straighten things out.

Think Total Service

Put yourself in your customers' shoes. What they expect from a product is that it will work as advertised and that you as the salesperson will stand behind it. But you can exceed their expectations by giving them even more. For example, one of my all-time favorite products is the Dictaphone. I carry two Dictaphones with me so I can dictate memos to my staff night and day. I actually dictate short little ideas into these Dictaphones all day long and leave the tapes for my secretary, Betty, who types them up and distributes them to the appropriate staffers. The thing I like most about this product is that the company has such a wonderful customer service and repair operation. I can run over my Dictaphone with my truck and they'll still repair it under warranty for me. I know that this is a product and a company that will be there for me in the future.

That's the sort of spirit you need to create for customers. And you do that by learning what customers expect and then giving them more.

RALPH'S RULE

Many salespeople try to "manage" expectations, but that's a mistake. You can't control customers' thoughts. Simply find out what they want and need. Then give them something over and above that. Pay particular attention to the softer or service side of the transaction.

Highs and Lows

I'm in my early 40s as I write this. When people ask me how old I am, maybe I'm vain because I sometimes tell them, "In six years I'll be in my 40s," which is true because I'll still be in my 40s at that time. But seriously, I've spent 23 years buying and selling real estate. And given the amount of success I've had—being named America's top-selling Realtor by *Time* magazine, doing 600 transactions a year when the average Realtor does about 10 per year—people look at me and think that my career must be one unbroken string of successes. Well, in this chapter I hope to show you that my career is probably a lot like yours—full of highs and lows—and that only my intensity level may be greater than yours. Elsewhere in this book, I'll give you ways to raise your career to new heights. But here I just want to remind you that we all face the same challenges.

Boy, have I had low days. Everyone remembers Babe Ruth as the greatest baseball player of all time, but not everyone recalls that he struck out more than anybody at the time, too. Despite being America's number-one Realtor I probably have failed to sell more houses than anybody. Because of my volume of business, I probably have been unable to sell more homes that I've listed than other Realtors have sold homes. My success and failure go hand in hand.

I'm not immune from making dumb mistakes, either, just like everyone else. I used to drive a Mercedes-Benz to show real estate in the late 1970s. In my part of metropolitan Detroit at that time, if you weren't driving an American car, you could not succeed in selling real estate. A lot of my potential customers were auto workers building Fords and Chryslers and GM cars. They'd take one look at me driving up in my foreign car and they'd want nothing to do with me. Or I'd park it somewhere and come back and there'd be scratches on the side. Today, with a more global economy and everything going so well in the economy, maybe it's different. But at the time I totally disregarded what other people knew because I was into showing off how successful I was. What a dope!

At the time I owned about a dozen rental properties. These were houses that I had bought as an investor to rent to other families. And I had just bought a nice house for myself, putting $20,000 down and agreeing to make $5,000 quarterly balloon payments in addition to the monthly payments, which I made directly to the seller under what in Michigan we call a land contract. Well, this was when interest rates hit 20 percent and my rental properties weren't producing any income and I was too proud to sell my car or move to a cheaper house.

Then the sellers of my house wanted to move back into it. They had retired to Florida and decided they didn't like Florida and didn't mind at all that I might be having trouble making my payments because they wanted the house back anyway. Try negotiating better terms with a former owner who wants the house back. No way, end of story.

So I lost my house to the former owner. For an ambitious guy like me, you can only imagine how bad I felt. It didn't end my career, of course. I got myself together, learned some lessons, and moved on. But my point is that I've made as many mistakes as anyone. I'm way ahead of the game but I wouldn't want anyone who reads this to imagine that my story is one of unbroken successes. And yours won't be, either. We all have our highs and lows.

But the lows shouldn't stop you from working hard. The harder you work and the more you learn from books like this one, the more success you'll have over the long run.

RALPH'S RULE

If you want a nice steady job with no surprises, stay out of sales. But if you're willing to see the highs and lows as part of the salesperson's life, and take them as just normal bumps in the road, you'll come out a winner.

My "Idea of the Week" Book

I'm a big believer in jotting down those random flashes of inspiration we all have. Well, actually, instead of physically writing anything down, I dicate ideas into my Dictaphones, as I described in a previous chapter.

A few years ago, I decided to create a system to involve my whole staff in this process. So I created my "Idea of the Week" book. I've subtitled mine "the greatest success generating tool" because that's what it is. I encourage all my staff to enter thoughts into it when they get good ideas. Everyone is encouraged to page through it from time to time and adapt whatever ideas they find useful.

For example, last month one of my top buyer agents, Paul Corona, wrote this:

"Old Idea but Good Idea: Having a great relationship with

another agent or two so you have the ultimate in teamwork when you are out of town or need assistance with a client." This ties into my system of referrals and teamwork around the office. We have started a buddy system whereby each new employee partners with someone for a while, not only to learn the ropes but to have someone to inspire him. Paul's idea was a reminder to all of us that lone-wolf salespeople can't do it all alone.

Sometimes the ideas are just simple little things to make life easier. A couple of winters ago someone wrote this: "Get salt spreader fixed and salt entire parking lot instead of shoveling salt." It was a reminder to me to take care of the everyday working conditions around my office.

At times the ideas are aimed at keeping me out of trouble. For example, since I'm pretty well known around my marketplace, a lot of candidates for government office ask me for money and endorsements. So during the 1996 election season my marketing specialist, Joe Hafner, wrote: "Don't publicly support political candidates. You could alienate too many people." It was a useful reminder to me to keep my business needs first.

A couple of years ago this suggestion turned up: "Make a checklist to put into buyer's package when meeting with them, a reminder about insurance, etc." Customers really appreciate any help we give them navigating the details of a transaction, so this was a very useful suggestion.

Another day, an employee named Mark reminded me that my "voice mail message should be upbeat—not regular. . . . Need enthusiasm!" You bet I followed up on this one right away!

This past winter, our in-house lawyer, Peter Allen, wrote: "Geri to do fax cover sheets for each salesperson/loan officer." Again, this wasn't a giant brainstorm but just a little idea to make us more efficient. But added together with all the other ideas we generate, it helps us achieve tremendous improvements in efficiency from year to year.

Starting an idea book is as simple as buying a notebook or journal and putting it in a prominent place in the office. Let everyone know they are free to jot down ideas and suggestions. They can sign their names or not as they choose. Discourage mere complaining that doesn't lead to useful changes. But by all means encourage your staff to think creatively, and not to be bashful about their ideas.

RALPH'S RULE

To achieve continuous improvement you must tap into everyone's creativity day to day and year to year. Creating a system to capture those flashes of inspiration will pay enormous dividends.

Flexibility Is Key

In the past few years I've gotten to know Marty Liebman, a part-ner in Media Power, an audio and visual production company here in metro Detroit. Marty's firm produces audio training tapes for me. I sell these tapes as one of my sales and motivational products. I've been so impressed by the flair that Marty brings to his work that I want to include him in this book.

Marty's family runs the respected Specs Howard School of Broadcast Arts here in metro Detroit. The school is where numerous professionals in television, radio, and advertising go for their training. Marty's own company, Media Power, offers a range of activities from training people on the latest editing equipment to producing commercials and training tapes.

But what most impresses me about Marty is that he relies, as I do, on a full range of activities and attitudes to succeed. So many lesser salespeople think they've got the one great secret of success, pumping all their efforts into a single marketing strat-egy, or refusing to add new product lines because their old one is so successful. Limiting yourself this way is misguided. In 23 years of selling real estate, I've revamped my business many times over, and I continue to do so today. Marty is the same, and his company is better for it.

Let's look at some of the ways.

Embracing New Technology

In a field as innovative as audio and visual production, Marty knows he has to buy the best. Both on the production side, where he's creating commercials and films on the latest digital editing equipment, and on the training side, working with students who expect to learn on the equipment they'll soon be using for real, Media Power keeps up by investing in the latest and best technology.

"Every time you turn around, there's something new out," Marty says. "You really do have to keep up." Clients expect Media Power to operate on the cutting edge, and they don't care if Marty invested a lot of money in what used to be the leading technology. "It's tough keeping up," Marty concedes. "You buy something, you turn around and it's obsolete." But there's no question Media Power gets its competitive edge from offering the very latest technology.

In your line of work, that could mean buying the latest programmable cellular phone to make your job easier. Or it could mean adding more fax machines in your office, as I've done. Or it could mean buying laptop computers for your sales staff. With laptops your salespeople can run through their marketing presentation in a customer's home or office at the touch of a few keystrokes.

Tending to Past Customers

People who follow my career know I'm a fanatic about keeping in touch with my past customers. A satisfied customer can be your customer for life. At this point in my career, I make a good living off the referrals and walk-in trade from my past client base. I keep up an aggressive marketing effort not because it's necessary to operate on my current level, but because I'm still trying to grow my business beyond this base. There's no question that past customers are worth all the trouble you lavish on them. It must take two or three times as much energy and effort to gain a new client as it does to service an existing one.

At Media Power, Marty says, "An awful lot of it is repeat business. You have to treat every client like they're your only client." Customers want to be treated well and they want to have a good relationship with a company like Media Power. Finding a new audio/visual production firm is difficult and you'd waste a lot of time if you changed production companies with each new project. So it's to everyone's benefit to keep the relationship in good shape. Marty understands this and goes out of his way to satisfy his repeat customers. He now has clients flying in from as far away as Ohio, Kentucky, and Missouri to do business with Media Power in Detroit.

Adapting to Changed Circumstances

Marty started out 10 years ago with just an audio production company. He did commercials for radio and similar products. Then he saw an opening to train production people in audio techniques. He added that piece of new business to his firm. Next, he entered a joint venture with the Specs Howard School to market a new line of digital editing systems. Soon he was training people for visual as well as audio production. Then he started dabbling in production himself, and that's been so successful that he's pushing the production end more heavily.

Media Power now offers a full range of audio and visual work—commercials, training films, audio tapes, editing, voice-over dubbing—the works. He's even won a Michigan Emmy award for one of his projects. He sets an example for all of us with his creative thinking and his ability to adapt to new opportunities.

Media Power actually employs just a small core staff. Marty hires a range of freelance writers and other professionals to supplement Media Power's staff on a project-by-project basis. This lets him stay flexible, another key to success.

Passion for the Work

My passion is selling, and Marty's is working with the latest audio and visual technology to satisfy clients. We're each totally committed to our careers. You need this kind of commitment to succeed. Only by believing completely in what you do will you have the energy to overcome the problems that arise every day.

In fact, if selling is a joy to you instead of a labor, you won't even notice many of the problems that stop lesser salespeople in their tracks.

RALPH'S RULE
Examples of success come in every field. But, like Marty, you need to employ a range of attitudes and techniques, not rely on just one.

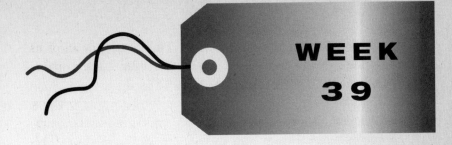

The Wrong and Right Ways to Manage Salespeople

About 10 years ago I decided to open my own sales company. Before that, I had always worked for others. During my earlier years I had had personal assistants working for me. But it was only when I opened my own company that I became a sales manager as well as doing my own sales.

At first, I made all the same dumb mistakes that most sales managers make. For example, I alienated my support staff. I didn't realize how left out they felt when I set up contests for our salespeople and would reward top producers with prizes and bonuses. I lost some good people. Today, I try to bring in the support people by getting them involved in the success of the company and rewarding them accordingly. They contribute through sales leads, suggestions, and the like. It's really made a difference—in the numbers, yes, but more so in the general office environment.

Another mistake I made: Money isn't everything. I found that if you rely primarily on cash and commissions to motivate your salespeople, you'll probably have success in the short term. But you'll lose your top people to your competition and you'll suffer high turnover in general. Salespeople crave recognition—it's all about ego for them. Bringing in $1 million is great, but the good ones care more about how they compare to their peers than how much they brought in. If they aren't recognized as part of an elite group, the dollar amount doesn't mean much—it has no value outside of the commission for them. If you want to turn salespeople into order takers, use a commission system as your sole reward system.

The best thing you can do is ask them how they want to be rewarded. Don't just promote them to sales managers. This is usually a waste of a good salesperson. In terms of ego, they will initially be pleased with the promotion and the increased power and responsibility. But you're taking them away from their strength—selling.

I'd ask a top person how he'd like to be rewarded. Maybe he wants to branch out to a different line of sales or she wants to personalize her reward system. One of my best people left me when I didn't understand that he wanted to sell fewer homes at higher prices, instead of my way, which involved more sales at lower prices. Actually our systems would have produced about the same revenue, but his was more efficient. When he saw my goals for him, he quit. He felt I had no idea what motivated him and what success meant to him. I goofed up. I didn't listen to him and what he wanted.

Sometimes you can reward people by giving them better tools to do their jobs. My secretary, Betty, once asked me for her own fax machine next to her desk so she wouldn't have to stand in line down the hall to fax a document. One of my buyer agents asked me for his own computer for his desk so he wouldn't have to share one. These are both top people and giving them these things was a no-brainer. It made them happier and even more productive.

To motivate people now, I do weekend getaways and contests. I put a lot of energy into recognition, including little things like thank-you notes. Also, I try to pull my people out of their sales cocoon. Recently, I assembled my staff and asked them all to do a collage that represented their goals. Pretty soon they were all clipping pictures and words out of magazines and pasting them on large sheets of poster boards. The point was to help them have a little fun and to just relax and be creative. Most people don't think they're creative, so they don't allow themselves to be. But part of being a good sales team is being creative and thinking outside your immediate surroundings. For example, when I go to sporting events, I always ask myself how I could get $10 from every person there. Some of my schemes are fairly ridiculous, but that isn't the point. It's a great game I play with myself to help keep my creative juices flowing.

Another big mistake that managers make: They often forget to manage and revert back to their sales behavior. You see this with people who have been promoted to manager when they never should have been or they simply haven't gotten the training they so desperately need.

This can happen when the salesperson brings them along to help seal a deal. In general, I think it's a great idea to bring along a sales manager in the final negotiations. It makes the client feel important, and the manager is supposed to make the salesperson look good in front of the client. I suggest it 100 percent. But it can backfire when the manager wants to hog the spotlight. The manager is so excited to be back in the middle of a sale that his ego wants all the attention. So he pushes the salesperson into the background.

How can the salesperson develop a relationship with the client when the client sees the salesperson as the second team? The manager is sabotaging his salesperson—and really bumming him out. He must remember that as the manager his job is to help his people achieve their goals. He has to change the way he thinks about success. It is no longer based on his own numbers, but on how good his team's numbers are. Taking this step back is tough for successful salespeople because they are so used to being hands-on.

I've made all these mistakes and more but I try to learn from my mistakes. I'm a better manager and motivator now than I was 10 years ago, and I hope to be even better tomorrow. You can be, too!

RALPH'S RULE

The key to good sales management is to realize that managing is different from selling. It requires different skills and a different view of what's important. Don't try managing unless you're willing to understand this difference.

My Presentation Folder

One of the themes of this book is that you always need to be just a little bit better and little bit different than your competition. Zillions of salespeople follow basically the same scripts when they go on a call. You need to find some way to separate yourself from that pack. One way I personally do that is with my presentation folder. Far from being just a catalog of products or services, my presentation folder delivers the story of my company and my own personal success. I believe it's essential to showing my potential customers what I've been able to achieve so far.

My presentation folder is a large-format zippered leather binder in which I have mounted photos of my family, a picture of my "U WIN" license plate, copies of awards or honors that I've received, even photos of my Corvette and of my wife and me in our hot tub at home. When I meet new clients I tell them my personal story, flipping through the pages of my folder to illustrate.

You may think that all this personal stuff doesn't sound appropriate for a sales call. But remember that most of my sales calls involve trying to get a listing to sell a home—a contract to represent a seller. Before sellers will give me that right, they must feel complete confidence in me. They have to believe that I'm the right person to whom they'll entrust their dreams. So my presentation folder is heavy on selling me as a person and as a success, and short on technical data about the marketplace.

You can always fill them in on the technical stuff later on. As I've said before, *people have to know you care before they care about what you know.*

I first developed my presentation folder years ago. I had noticed that a lot of times I would go to appointments and walk away thinking, "If I had just said this or that I would have gotten the order." Some days you're on, some days you're off. To correct for those bad days or lapses of memory, my presentation keeps me focused and lets me cover all the things I want to cover. My presentation evolves and changes all the time as my circumstances change, but it always focuses on me and my family and our success story.

Today, I'm training all my assistants to develop their own presentation folders. These folders will tell the story of our team as well as of the individual salesperson. I supply them with the leather folders and many of the inserts. For example, I believe it helps my customers to feel confidence in us if they know I've written one and now a second book on salesmanship. So I include the jacket covers from both *Walk Like a Giant, Sell Like a Madman* and now this new book in everyone's presentation folder.

My customers, like people everywhere, like to see happy things—weddings, babies, people having a good time. Even if they're divorced, it still makes them feel good to see photos of people at a wedding. So I have lots of family photos in my presentation folder. I'll show them a photograph of my ring, which has the letters SOLD in gold, and then I'll show them the ring itself and tell them that that's what I want to do for their home. I try to get people laughing and emotionally involved in the decision to let me be their salesperson. We may think that competition has reduced everything merely to a question of price, but that's not true. Customers will always respond better to a salesperson who's warm and funny and honest with them than to one who is cold and technical.

So I have photos of my daughter during her karate lessons and one of me in a greaser group I belonged to in the 1980s. We'd slick back our hair and wear leather jackets and go out and do charitable work. There's a photo of my Corvette and photos of the foreign exchange students who have lived with us. There's also a photo and story about me that appeared a few years ago in *Time* magazine. And people will say, "Yeah, I remember seeing Ralph on the cover of *Time*." Well, I wasn't on the cover, I was inside the magazine, but I don't correct people. I just let it flow.

While I don't get too technical in my folder, I do include promotional material about our title company and our mortgage company, and checklists and order forms to make any transaction go more smoothly.

My presentation folder also includes referral forms. During each listing call, I give my potential customers a referral sheet and ask them to refer at least one other person to me. And if they do so right away, that's great. That's a little yes on the way to giving you the big yes when they give you their order. No matter what you sell—airplanes, boats, cars, real estate—you've always got to ask for referrals. Now, when I say always, bear in mind that if you're in a tense situation with a customer who is making excessive demands on you, you may not want his business. And you probably shouldn't ask for a referral then, because people tend to refer people like themselves. But, generally, you always want to ask for referrals and have a sheet ready so a customer can fill out the referral form right there.

In the past couple of years, I've loaded my complete presentation onto a laptop computer, which I take with me on sales calls.

But I always carry my leather presentation folder, too. The reason is that some people respond better to the high-tech approach. When I get inside someone's house, I'll look around and if there's a lot of technology present, I'll take my notebook computer out of my briefcase, plug it in, and dazzle them with my presentation that way. But if I get a sense my customer would be put off by too slick a show, I'll use my presentation folder, which has a nice broken-in look to it.

Speaking of technology, when I first created my presentation folder in the late 1980s, I was one of the first entrepreneurs who owned a fax machine. So I included a photo of my fax machine and one of my Dictaphone, just to show people that I was keeping up to date with the latest technology to help me sell their home faster and better.

Gradually, I move the discussion during a presentation into the guts of the deal. I'll explain the different ways in which I'll list and market their home. I'll talk about the closing process and lock boxes that basically let us show their home when they're away. I talk about all the things I can do to make their life easier during this transition period. I tell them about my mortgage company and how I can guarantee that a tentative agreement to buy their home will never fall through because the buyer wasn't financially qualified. I couldn't make that guarantee as recently as a year ago because my mortgage company was still getting organized, but now I can.

It may take me an hour to go through my entire presentation. I've gotten the time down over the years. I've streamlined things and I've gotten better at giving my presentation. You may not have an hour to devote to a presentation, but whatever time you do have, use it to establish some emotional rapport with the customer. If you start out talking strictly about price or some other technical consideration, the customer feels no pain when they walk away from you. But after a Ralph Roberts–style presentation, my customers at least know they'd being saying no to a real person just like them who has a family and a home and friends.

In short, my presentation folder is another system I've developed to help me focus on what's important during the sales call. I know it makes me more efficient, and thus more successful. Maybe you're in the kind of selling job where a presentation folder isn't practical—say, selling shoes in a mall outlet. But I bet you there are millions of Americans who sell Amway products, or real estate, or something else who could benefit from creating their own presentation books.

RALPH'S RULE
A presentation book is a great way to get your potential clients enjoying the sales call instead of dreading it.

When to Fire a Customer

When you're struggling to do deals in a competitive marketplace, you may think that you could never "fire" a customer. Letting go of a deal voluntarily seems crazy. After all, you probably think you're killing yourself just to find new ones. Sometimes, though, you have to say no to deals. In fact, turning down a deal that's wrong for you may be one of the best skills you learn from this book.

Let me give you an example from my own business. Recently, we had a house listed that needed a price reduction. (A listing is the contract between seller and agent that lets the salesperson represent the home for a given amount of time.) It was listed at $159,000 and I knew that the price needed to be reduced to about $139,000 in order to sell. The homeowner resisted the price reduction. Making things worse was the interference from another agent who was telling my customer it should be priced even higher than $159,000. We argued with him for three days. We had a six-month listing agreement, and we were two months into it. I knew this house wasn't going to sell in that market at the higher price.

Well, I'd rather give it up today than let him down in the next four months. So that's what I did. I thanked the customer for the business but told him I thought another agent would be a better match for him. And I walked away from it.

This is a skill I learned years ago. My wife, Kathy, said to me about 10 years ago that I was spending too much time on certain deals. She'd say, "Ralph, you've spent 10 hours on this file this month. Wouldn't it make sense to take that same time, go out and get five more listings, and let this one go?" And she was right. Part of being a successful salesperson is recognizing which deals to concentrate on and which to let go.

Here's my advice: If you have five deals that you're working, figure out which one gives you the most trouble and let that one go. You will automatically get more business, because now you will be able to work more productively instead of spinning your wheels. You can play offense instead of defense.

Having a customer with unrealistic demands is just one reason to make the painful decision to give a customer the heave-ho. Here are a few more:

You Can't Deliver

Sometimes you may not have the product the customer needs, or you're stretched too thin. In those cases you may be tempted to keep the deal anyway, but remember the downside. If you can't deliver on your promises, you've lost that customer permanently. Even worse, the bad reputation you may get in your industry will hamper all your future efforts. When you can't deliver what you say, drop the deal before you get started.

The Customer Is Too Negative

The old saying about the customer always being right doesn't mean you have to put up with abusive comments or an extremely negative environment. Sometimes a customer distrusts salespeople from the get-go. Sometimes he may have had a bad experience with a salesperson and he's going to take it out on you.

When you find yourself dealing with a negative, abusive customer, evaluate how important this deal is to you. Obviously, if your production level is high, it's easier to walk away from a deal that's draining your energies. But even if you're struggling to get started, it may be right to drop someone who is consistently abusive or argumentative. After all, you're there to help people, not make enemies. For every nasty customer, there are dozens more nice people who can use your services.

When the Deal Doesn't Fit Your Business Plan

I hope you are making out a business plan. When I put mine together, I'm very specific about what kinds of deals I'm going to do and where I'm going to concentrate my efforts. If I find myself getting drawn into a deal that doesn't fit my plan, or one that I know will only distract me from my longer-term goals, I turn it down.

To take a simple example, let's say you've been selling in the lower price range of your industry. Your goal is to move into a higher price range. Well, then, you should concentrate on developing customers in the higher price range. You'll still get calls from your old marketplace, but you'll have to decide when to let those go to free you to pursue your new goals.

RALPH'S RULE

Turning down business may sound like insanity to a struggling salesperson. But saying no is a vital skill. Once you develop a strong customer base, try to develop some judgment about which deals to keep and which to let go. It'll pay off for you in the long run.

Don't Add It Up!

Many years ago, I was driving to what I was sure would be my biggest commission check ever. I was selling a restaurant. Normally I didn't do commercial real estate deals, just residential homes. But I was doing this one, and it sounded like a sure-fire deal for me. My commission was going to be $20,000—a heck of a lot of money for somebody of my age and experience. On the way to the closing I got caught in a traffic jam and I turned on the car radio. I was listening to the news. Imagine how sick I felt when I heard that the restaurant I was about to close on was engulfed in flames. There went my commission up in smoke. The owners never rebuilt, either. They eventually sold the land and the new owner put up a McDonald's.

Before I heard the news, I had been planning how to spend that $20,000. I had it all mapped out—every penny. I know now that I was committing one of the prime errors of the sales profession. Losing that commission taught me a valuable lesson: Don't add it up in advance!

The worst thing you can do as a salesperson is add up pending sales. I catch people doing that all the time. A lot of salespeople will tell themselves, "If I can only close this deal I'll have this much money . . ." But some deals fall apart, and if you add it up in advance, you'll never make the total.

Say you have 10 deals pending this month. And say each deal will net you a commission of $1,000. So you're looking at a $10,000 monthly income—not bad if it comes true. But say you average one or two lost deals per month. That $10,000 that you've been counting turns out to be only $8,000—a 20 percent drop. Suddenly, the extra rewards you were counting on can no longer happen. Your sense of disappointment may get the better of you and send you into a tailspin.

Let's not forget that when typical commission salespeople fall behind in their income, they have to borrow from others to pay their bills. This often results from poor planning or no planning at all. Clearly you need to work out a budget and stick to it, especially in your early years when you're starting out. You should have a rough idea what your income will be, but what I'm saying in this chapter is you shouldn't *count on* any one given deal until it's actually closed.

Besides, I've noticed that salespeople who add up the profits in advance tend to quit too early. They make their quota at mid-month and then they coast until the next sales period. What a waste! Salespeople who are good enough to reach their monthly goals early should keep pushing ahead. Think how much more money they'd make that way.

Adding it up in advance is one of the easiest habits to fall into—and one of the most destructive for salespeople. Don't do it! The people who add it up in advance are almost always the ones who strike out.

RALPH'S RULE

Get in the habit of concentrating on closing your deals—not on the profits they promise. Work the deals first and the profits will follow.

Why Size *Doesn't* Matter

I'm five feet, 11 inches, and my brother, Dave, also a top-producing real estate salesman, is four feet, 11 inches. I sell homes in a working-class suburb of Detroit; Dave sells homes in a single exclusive subdivision at the Royal Palm Yacht and Country Club in Boca Raton, Florida. I show customers homes from my Chevy Suburban; Dave shows homes to customers from a golf cart.

My point here is that these superficial differences don't matter. Dave and I both rank among the most successful real estate salespeople in our profession. Why? Because the sales techniques that I use in Detroit are the same that Dave uses in Boca Raton. The attention to detail, the importance of marketing and self-promotion, the tending to the needs of past customers—all these count whether your sales are big or small, or whether you're selling cars or cosmetics.

Sometimes people tell me, "Oh, I know you're successful, but your methods won't work in my field." To which I reply, baloney. The techniques of good salesmanship have been proven over and over. It's up to you to learn them and apply them.

I have many friends who are marketing or account executives with large corporations. On the surface, their markets couldn't be more different from mine. Most of my deals close fairly quickly; their deals may take a year to conclude. My marketplace includes modestly priced houses; they may be dealing with a typical contract worth $5 million to $50 million. I deal with a single customer, or a married couple; they must often work their way through 20 layers of corporate management to close a sale.

Yet despite these differences, selling to large corporations requires the same techniques that I use to sell homes. Among them:

Stay Visible

The best corporate account execs use mass mailings to let their customers know they're in business. These may include a cover letter and a brochure or some other material. Just as I use letters, brochures, flyers, and other types of mail describing what's happening in my market and what I can do for customers, corporate marketing people do essentially the same. In the fiercely competitive world of corporate sales, letting your customer know you're in business becomes crucial.

Staying it touch with clients remains absolutely critical to your success. The more of this you do, the better. I often send as many as a dozen mailings a year to each potential client in my marketplace. As I've said many times, people can't buy from me if they don't know I'm in business.

Avoid Manipulative Techniques

A lot of people who don't object to the salesperson or his product may balk at being manipulated. When I was a young salesperson, I attempted to sell homes by dazzling my customers with my scripted remarks, jokes, etc. These canned approaches usually fail—as they should. You're in business to help clients, and you can't do that by using some corny script that you've read in a magazine. You've got to learn to listen and move the sale forward by drawing out the customer's true needs and concerns.

Most senior corporate buyers are sophisticated enough to spot any canned approach from a mile away. It's not the salesperson as an individual that they object to; it's the arrogant assumption that someone can be coerced or manipulated into buying through the use of scripted remarks or other devices.

Find the True Decision Maker

When corporate account reps make their multiple presentations at various levels of a corporation, they have to discern where the true power lies. In a multitiered corporation, often different levels exercise different levels of power. The technical people may act as gatekeepers on quality-control issues; the finance people may raise questions based on expected rates of return. You've got to learn who the decision makers are at each level and learn what they want and need from the product or service.

It's no different when I sell homes. Except that instead of selling to 20 levels of a corporate hierarchy, I'm selling to a wife and husband at their kitchen table. But even when dealing with a couple, I still have to learn who actually makes the decisions, and what issues are most important to that person.

There are many other points of similarities between my accounts and corporate selling. Salespeople at all levels must know their product thoroughly; they must understand their industry; they must educate themselves continuously on developments in their field. They need to understand the dollar value of each daily activity and they must concentrate on the most important dollar-productive ones. They need to delegate the nonessential paperwork chores to assistants to free themselves to do what they do best.

These are the essentials of salesmanship. It makes no difference what kind of product you sell or what industry you're in. If you do the basics well, you will be successful.

RALPH'S RULE

Don't be fooled into thinking that lessons from more successful salespeople don't apply to you. Success is just a matter of adapting their techniques to your own situation.

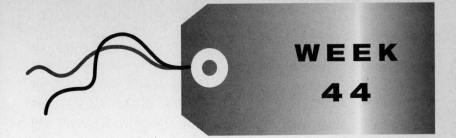

Building Wealth Through Investing

It's the goal of almost every salesperson to get rich. Getting rich for most of us means more than selling. It also means investing our money and making it grow. Not just "watching" it grow by parking it in a mutual fund or something like that. We want to *make* it grow by actively investing in real estate or small businesses or in some other entrepreneurial venture. In this chapter, I'll tell you a little about how I do that.

For me, the more visible part of my business—the listing and selling of homes—is only part of what I do. I also own right now about 300 investment properties. I'm an investor in a mobile home park. I have my own mortgage company. I buy, renovate, and sell HUD and VA foreclosure properties. I have my own title company, too. I'm involved in condominium projects and various other projects. All of these combine with my basic real estate business to make me successful.

Most people who call or talk to me want to know how they can get started. It's a great question. The answer is to surround yourself with smart people. There are experts in every field, and many of them are willing to help you out. You may think that these experts are your competitors and that they may not be willing to share their secrets with you. In fact, you may run into a few people like that. But there are many others who are happy to share their wealth-building secrets with you. Take me. No matter how rich I become, I'll never be able to buy all the investment properties in the world or do all the real estate transactions. My goal is to grow my company from 600 transactions a year to 1,000, but even that would be just a tiny fraction of all the real estate deals in metro Detroit. I can afford to help others achieve their dreams by sharing my ideas.

So first I'd join some sort of investors' group. There are investment property owners associations, stock clubs, and other types of investment groups. You can probably find referrals in the local paper or on the Internet or perhaps by listening to one of the local radio shows that offer investment advice. The key is to associate yourself with people who are successfully doing what you want to be doing. Talk to the people there. Often these groups meet once or twice a month. Success leaves big footprints, and the experts are usually willing to share their wisdom with you.

In this way you'll begin to get the expert advice you need. This can work no matter what level you're at today. Let me tell you a story about Mark Victor Hansen, author of the Chicken Soup for the Soul series of books. Mark and I are working on one of these books about people who have disabilities. Mark told me once how he had asked the personal power guru Anthony Robbins how to increase his wealth. For several years, Mark had been making "only" a few million with no increase in revenue. Robbins told him he was in that "rut" because he associated only with people who made a few million a year. If he wanted to make $20 million a year, he needed to hang out with people making that much. As wild as that may sound, I think it's good advice. Certainly it's true that if you want to get going as an investor, you need to find successful investors to be around and model yourself after.

Your other big need as a beginner will be capital. To raise investment capital, you have to find people who believe in you. It's okay to start small. I describe elsewhere in this book how I took $900 from my high school graduation money and used it as a down payment for my first home. My grandmother loaned me money many times. My family lawyer, who has known me for 30 years, has given me cash to invest more times than I can count.

Over the years, people have given me literally millions of dollars to invest for them. Sometimes these are people who want me to buy houses for them. Maybe it'll be one per year, or maybe 10 per year. They let me know when they're ready to buy and then I find them something fairly quickly. Some of my investors may prefer only a little amount of risk, so I'll give them a first position at a lower rate of return. Recently, I've been talking with two banks about creating a $12 million real estate fund to help me expand my investments even more.

Several years ago, a group of investors and I developed a mobile home park. Approximately 400 people pay over $300 a month to rent lot space. The investors and I don't have many expenses, mostly insurance and operational things. This project worked out about as perfectly as any of my deals ever has. There is little overhead and a good cash flow. After it was finished, we were able to borrow on it more than the $2 million that it had cost us to develop it. These kinds of deals are out there—you just have to be around other investors who do them.

It's a far cry from my earliest days when I used my initial $900 to get started. But once you demonstrate that you have some expertise in your field, you should be able to raise additional money to make more investments. And that, in turn, will lead to more investment capital. You may make mistakes, as I have. But I persevered through it all and continued to find family, friends, and investors who believed in me and my dreams.

You can build wealth, too, if you associate with good people. I learned a long time ago that if you want to be a good salesperson, you've got to hang out with other good salespeople. If you want to be a good husband and father, hang with other good husbands and fathers. You'll pick up many ideas and positive attitudes just by being with these people who have already achieved what you've only dreamed of doing.

RALPH'S RULE

Building wealth is not magic. It's a steady process of learning from the experts and using what funds you have today to build greater wealth for tomorrow.

Problem Solving for Your Customers

One of the most frequent problems my customers bring to me is how can they save enough money for a down payment on a house. Ability to pay is a recurring problem in any line of sales; but most salespeople don't spend enough time helping their customers solve this problem. Many salespeople, faced with a customer who really can't afford their product, will do one of two things: They'll turn away in indifference, or they'll sell them the product anyway without any regard for their financial well-being. Both those approaches are wrong.

In this chapter, I want to illustrate how we need to get creative to solve our customers' problems. Why? Because a customer you help today will be your customer tomorrow. If you sell a client something she doesn't need or can't afford, you may book one commission. But what a waste! Pretty soon that customer realizes that she's in over her head, and she'll blame you, and you know what? She's right. Salespeople should never put their own financial well-being ahead of that of customers.

So how do you get creative to help your customers? The most important element is to know your product and your industry inside out. Once you understand all the elements of a deal, you'll be able to reach for the right solution. After 23 years helping people realize their dream of home ownership, I can help almost any buyers, no matter how short of cash, no matter how bruised their credit, buy a house.

Let me give you a few examples to show you what I mean. For example, when I have customers who can't afford a down payment, I may suggest they borrow from a 401(k). They have to be careful, though, as you can borrow only one loan at a time from a 401(k). So if they use this method, I tell them to borrow enough, because they can't go back until the first loan is repaid.

Another way is to ask the seller to pay closing costs. This is a highly popular method here in Michigan and one that I've used in my deals many, many times. Once sellers realize that the deal will go more smoothly and quickly if they contribute a little to the transactions costs, they usually agree. And, under the right circumstances, the seller can even deduct those costs from taxes.

A third way is to set up a wedding trust. Many first-time home buyers are newly married, and with a little planning they can accept gifts from friends as well as relatives toward the purchase of a home. Again, you have to be careful of the rules; check with your banker or lawyer about setting one up. But it's a great way for others to contribute to your happiness. I predict that in a few years these wedding trust plans will become a much more common way of financing a home.

Yet another way is to borrow up to 20 percent of the total cost from the seller. In this case, you in effect ask the seller to forgo accepting the down payment now. Instead, the seller agrees to wait, say, five years for the payment, at which point the buyer refinances the house, using the equity gained to pay the seller. Perhaps in a very hot home-buying market this method wouldn't be popular. But at a time when homes aren't selling quite so fast, this is a great way for sellers to get nearly all they want and for buyers to get into a home.

There are yet more ways to solve the problem of a down payment. I've gone on at some length about this because I want to illustrate that there are many things you can do to help your customers. I'm sure you can come up with any number of creative solutions in your own industry, whether you sell trains, planes, or automobiles.

If you know something about real estate, you may think my list of solutions was fairly obvious. But you'd be surprised at the number of Realtors who have *never* suggested *even one* of these methods to their more needy buyers. That's a shame. I believe that many, many deals never get done not because the buyers can't afford the price, but because the salesperson hasn't been creative enough.

A salesperson who works only on the easy deals is nothing more than an order taker. A real salesperson is one who makes something good happen when the customer's well-being is on the line.

RALPH'S RULE

A salesperson is more than a mere agent for a product or service. A true salesperson is a problem solver. That's where we find our greatest satisfactions and our greatest rewards.

Dealing with the Competition

Realtors, Amway representatives, car salespeople, stockbrokers, and even parents who are trying to sell their kids on the idea of doing their homework all have something in common. We're all salespeople, and one of the truisms of selling is that all salespeople face competition. You daughter may counter your demand that she go to bed by pointing out that her favorite program is on or that her friend doesn't have to go to bed as early as she does. You can just pull rank and order her to go to bed, but at some point you'll need to counter her objections, and that's where dealing with the competition comes in.

Moreover, competition in most types of selling is getting tougher than ever. The big auto manufacturers are actually shutting down 10 to 20 percent of dealerships around the country to streamline their distribution channels. Information available on the Internet is turning more and more sales of all products into merely a question of price. There are probably about 600,000 people actively selling real estate in America today, and half of them will leave the business within five years due to competition.

If you want to be one of the hardy ones who survive and thrive in this brave new world, you've got to know how to separate yourself from your competitors.

We do this in all kinds of ways. For example, some of my customers are people who are deciding between buying an existing home that I represent and buying a new home from a builder. And, obviously, the newly built homes have lots of advantages. It's very tempting to walk through a model home and see how clean it looks and start to dream about owning one just like it.

To deal with this threat, first of all I'll try to outdo the competition in this regard. I'll get my home sellers to make their house as much like a model home as possible. I tell families when I'm selling their home to clear away all the clutter and give stuff away or throw stuff away and make their home look spotless, as if no one lives there. This goes a long way toward reducing the gap with my builder competitors.

I'll also describe to my potential buyer what the replacement cost of this house would be if you had to build it all over again. The replacement cost may be $350,000 but this one is on the market for $279,900. This helps underscore the value of my product. I'll also point out that a buyer doesn't need to wait for the builder to finish the new house in six months because the home I represent is on the market right now. Or, I'll show the buyer that the newly built home may not have a lawn-sprinkling system built in but my house does have one.

In other words, I make my product as attractive as possible to lessen any possible advantage a buyer may see in a different product. You can do this in many ways. If you're selling home products of the kind where every representative sells basically the same stuff, you can succeed by getting your prospects excited about dealing with you instead of someone else. It sounds simple to say this, but you accomplish it through all those things that salespeople are supposed to be doing—staying in touch and probing for the customer's concerns about the product and always, always making sure the customer knows you're in business and ready to sell.

One thing you should not do is badmouth your competition. It reflects badly on you and it will always hurt you in the end.

Sometimes you'll run into the tricky situation where you have to give bad news to a client, like your product costs more than your competitor's. Even in these cases, don't be afraid to share information with your clients, as so many salespeople are. Your product or service probably has advantages that your competitor's product lacks. Pointing out why something else is cheaper allows you to point out why your higher price makes sense.

Remember, even if your product and price are virtually identical to those of the competition, you can still stand out through a little showmanship and customer service. You may not control details of price, but you can exceed the competition in how you treat your customers. That's where true success lies anyway. Just continue to work your plan and not worry so much about what others are doing.

RALPH'S RULE

You can't change what your competitors are doing but you can make your own presentation better. Work on improving your own customer skills rather than fretting about everyone else.

Positive Talking

The first date I ever went on with my wife, Kathy, was to lunch at a local pancake house. I had met Kathy when I was running one of my sports bars and she and her girlfriends came in. At first she didn't seem very interested in me. I tried to spark her interest in various ways without much success. Then, after talking on the phone a few times, I finally said that we should have lunch at the pancake house, and would she like me to pick her up or meet me there? And that's what finally got us going together.

Notice I didn't ask Kathy, "Would you like to have lunch with me?" My question assumed we were having lunch, and the only question was how to get there. This is an example of asking for something in a way that assumes a positive outcome. I've heard this technique called "power talking" and various other terms. It's a tried-and-true sales technique, as when a waitress asks, "Would you like a glass of red or white?" instead of "Would you like a glass of wine?" But, like most of the techniques in this book, it's one that too many salespeople ignore.

Recently, on a very busy day when I hardly had time to think, a reporter began a telephone interview with me asking if she could tape record our conversation. Instead of just saying, "Yeah, that's okay," I replied, "Get out your tape recorder and let's have some fun!" She laughed and I could just feel her energy level rising. The interview continued on this higher level of energy, and that, of course, resulted in a more positive story for me.

Basically, positive talking is a way to emphasize common ground, to create positive thinking, and to get both sides working toward a successful outcome. It's a way to express your interest in your client's well-being. It's a way to energize a situation. Just think how the singing of the National Anthem before a baseball game energizes the crowd. You want that same quick uplift in energy when you begin a sales call. Positive talking can help you get that.

Picture this: Suppose you go into a meeting after a long, difficult day. You're grouchy and tired, and you don't really want to be there. When your host says, "How are you?" you could be bluntly honest and say what kind of day you've had. Or you could say, "Great! And this meeting will make my day even better." The second version is more likely to lift your own spirits and put everyone in the mood to do business.

Here I'll draw a distinction between this upbeat, forward-looking style of conversing and a reliance on scripts or other phony approaches. You can't rely on scripted remarks without putting off your clients. They can tell when you're not sincere. Positive talking doesn't mean being phony or dishonest or manipulative.

Rather, being positive assumes you still react honestly to any given situation but that you remain confident, focused, and engaged with the client in your conversational style. Positive talking is a way of conversing that increases the energy level for both you and your client, while negative talking drains away that energy. Positive talking alone won't win you a new client, but the lack of it will lose you many.

RALPH'S RULE

Pay careful attention to your conversational style with clients. Ask yourself this: Would you want to do business with you? Customers like salespeople who are positive and professional and who make them feel special. Positive talking can help you achieve this image.

Just Do It!

One of my acquaintances, Pat Donofrio, is a judge in the local court system. No matter what opinion you hold about lawyers, salespeople could learn a lot from this particular judge about good work habits. I know I have. And I'd like to share Pat's story with you.

Like that of most judges, Pat's docket is jammed with cases. When he became a judge in early 1997, his circuit had a five-year backlog of civil litigation. Pat believes in the old saying that justice delayed is justice denied. He makes it his business to stay at work until he has accomplished everything to stay current.

That has meant holding court at night and on weekends. It also means turning around the policy of granting unlimited delays in lawsuits. Instead, Pat likes to call the parties into his chambers, talk out the issues in a dispute, and keep the parties talking to each other until they agree on a settlement.

"My view is the clock doesn't have enough hours in it," Pat told me. "The way to lead is by example and that translates into hard work. I used to run my law firm the same way. If you want subordinates to work hard, you have to show them that work is valued and that you work hard yourself."

In most of this book, I've been teaching you ways to work smarter. But sometimes, salespeople have to follow Judge Donofrio's example and work harder as well as smarter. As Nike says, "Just do it!"

The rewards will come. For salespeople, working harder usually means making more money. In many ways, sales remains a numbers game. Up to a point, the more people you contact, the more sales you'll have.

I say "up to a point" because there are limits to hard work. When I was a younger man, I routinely worked 100-hour weeks. My goal was to get home before the end of *Nightline*, which aired at about 11:30 P.M. in Detroit. I was obsessed with my job for years. The result is that I almost killed myself with a poor diet, too much work, and never seeing my family. I admit I wasn't there enough for my oldest daughter, Kolleen, when she was younger.

In recent years, I've managed to tame this obsession. Now I have what I describe as a healthy passion for sales. I work probably 60 hours a week and schedule regular time off for my family and friends.

But if you're in sales and you're working 40 hours a week, you're leaving money behind on the table. No one can work 40 hours a week and make all the sales calls and handle the paperwork and do networking and self-promotion. You may be able to get away with working 40 hours a week occasionally, but other times you'll have to put in longer hours to achieve what you need to do.

Working harder is especially important when you face a major backlog, as Pat Donofrio did. "The best way is to roll up your sleeves and get to work," he says.

By the way, Pat found that working harder also had a positive effect on the lawyers and parties to lawsuits. When they found out that he intended to keep them there until they settled, or to go to trial in the near future, it concentrated their minds on the problem. It led to quicker, and better, decision making. The whole process got more efficient. Remember how the O. J. Simpson trial lasted more than a year? As I write this, Pat just completed his 38th trial in 54 weeks.

Just as you should involve your customers and employees in your hard work, Pat tries to get the parties to a suit to really understand what's behind his efforts. "I want them to buy into the process of reaching a resolution. I think it's important that litigants feel part of that process, not that it's just two lawyers talking to the judge in his chambers."

Recently, for example, two lawyers came in, each seeking a restraining order against the other's client. It was a typical business dispute. Many judges would have routinely granted one or the other order or both. But, Pat says, "I don't just sign orders." Instead, he called the clients into his chambers and spent two hours exploring the case. By the end of that time, the parties were ready to put a settlement agreement on the record.

"The sooner you get to the central issues, the sooner you can get to a resolution," Pat says.

What I hope you take away from this chapter is a commitment to clearing away your own backlogs. And to keep you focused on that goal, here are some tips for working smarter while you work harder.

Plan

Nothing focuses you on the essential tasks as well as daily and weekly planning. Each morning I take 15 minutes and make entries in my Franklin planner on what I want to accomplish that day. I put in personal as well as business goals. Once I put down all the tasks, I prioritize them so I know what to do first. It's my way, as Pat says, to get to the central issues.

Without planning, you'll bounce from crisis to crisis with no idea what you should be doing next. Without planning, you'll be working longer hours but getting less done. I predict that if you work the same number of hours you do now, but add 15 minutes of daily planning, you'll see an increase in your sales and profits.

Delegate

One of my keys to success has been learning to delegate. In his courtroom, Pat has someone to assist him, and of course there are many employees in the court clerk's office to keep track of the voluminous files. In the same way, I've always had assistants, right from the very beginning. When I was a 19-year-old novice just entering sales, I hired a teenage co-op student to answer the phones for me after school. I had my own secretary and several personal assistants handling paperwork for me long before it was fashionable in the real estate industry. In fact, one of the reasons that more Realtors have assistants today is that I popularized the idea in the 1980s and early 1990s.

Delegation frees you to spend your time on the really important stuff—meeting with customers, networking, and strategic planning for the future.

Use Technology to Leverage Your Efforts

Today's court system couldn't run without computers. In the same way, I've always invested in new technology to gain an edge. I use everything from a satellite route-finding system in my sport utility vehicle to more traditional things like the Dictaphone. Each type of technology either multiplies my efforts or enables me to concentrate on what's important.

For example, my satellite navigation system in my Chevy Suburban frees me from worrying over directions. I just type in my destination and the system directs me, right down to telling me where to turn and when. I have always found that technology buys me free hours to devote to actual selling. Some new piece of technology may cost a lot, but the new transactions I do more than pay for my investment.

Know When to Take a Break

There comes a time when every salesperson hits the wall of exhaustion. Whether it happens to you at 60 hours a week or 100 hours a week, learn to recognize the symptoms. If your family complains about never seeing you, if problems in the office leave you edgy all the time, if your production seems to be leveling off or even falling no matter how hard you work, it's time to take some time off. You'll come back feeling refreshed and ready to work again.

But don't use your need for a break to justify slacking off when you should be selling. I think more sales are lost around the water cooler and the coffee machine than just about anywhere else. Patricia Tripp, a British hairdresser who became an internationally famous motivational speaker, says she used to view lunch hour as a time to squeeze in three more appointments. That's my advice, too.

Work smarter, yes, but work harder, too.

Case closed.

RALPH'S RULE

Don't go into sales if you don't want to work hard. There may be limits to this approach, but generally the harder you work, the more money you will make.

Breaking the Sales Slump

More than 50 million Americans are now in sales, either in home-based businesses or in a career selling cars or trucks, real estate, mortgages, clothing, you name it. And of those 50 million salespeople, probably 40 million of them, or 80 percent of the entire field, at any one time are in a sales slump. A slump can last an hour, a day, a week, a month, or even longer. These slumps may be inevitable, but if you want to stay in sales as a career, you cannot sit back and wait for better days to come. You've got to take deliberate steps to break out.

Some of the following steps have helped me and others I have coached and trained emerge from a sales slump:

Avoid Negative People and Situations

There is nothing worse that talking about negative situations in the workplace. Avoid the water cooler or coffee room where people moan all day about how terrible things are. To break out of a slump you need all your positive energy. Talking about bad stuff will only bring you down just when you need to feel great.

Set a Start Date

Do it cold turkey. Break your sales slide by getting back to the basics. You may want to increase the number of new daily contacts you make from 25 to 50 or even 100. There's nothing like taking decisive action for breaking out of a slow period.

Be Committed

Breaking the sales slump is not easy, but it can be done. Continue to be committed. Once you recognize that you are in a sales slump you can begin to initiate change. You also realize you have had these setbacks before and will probably have them again.

Make Marketing a Regular Activity

If you make marketing a routine activity, something you do in good times and bad, you'll find that your slumps come less frequently and don't last as long. It's the salespeople who ignore marketing when times are good and do it only when times are bad who find their sales valleys deeper and longer.

You Must Keep Records

I encourage you to get involved in some day planning system such as the wonderful Franklin planner system that I use. To be successful you must be able to go back and look at a certain week, certain day, certain time frame and say why your units or sales weren't what you wanted them to be. Perhaps you weren't making your prospecting calls the week before or perhaps you spent too much time on paperwork and not enough meeting customers. Records will tell you that.

Talk to Your Manager About Your Sales Decline

If management doesn't bring it up, approach your manager. Chances are your manager may have some ideas about what's wrong. At the very least, talking through the problem may relieve the feeling of isolation that comes with a slump.

Learn from Past Mistakes

Think about what helped you in the past. Think about what hurt you in the past.

Get Your Family and Friends Involved

Make it a contest. For example, tell them that if you're the top salesperson of the month, the following month you'll take them to a theme park for a long weekend. If you're the top salesperson of the week, the family gets to go out to dinner. Getting your family excited about your success will motivate them to motivate you with their support and suggestions.

You Have to Learn to Cope!

You have to learn that there are sales slumps. You will get out of them. They will happen again. I have my sales slumps under such control that I can feel them. In the middle of the day, I get up from my desk, walk around the office, and tell myself that I just have to make things happen.

RALPH'S RULE
Slumps are inevitable, but they don't have to come as often or last as long as you think they might.

My Worst Day Ever

The day I'll tell you about in this chapter happened just a few weeks ago as I write this. I've had lots of hectic and disappointing days in my 23 years selling real estate. But I don't think I've ever had one where so many unfortunate things piled on me one after the other. Of course, as a salesperson, I tend to be carried away by my emotions. My wife and staff were able to point out days worse than the one I'm about to describe. But I had already put those days behind me, just as I'll soon put this day behind me. I mean, I've lost a home in foreclosure, had a controller who stole $80,000 from me, had a house I owned burn down without insurance, and countless other disasters that could easily qualify as my "worst day ever." In fact, I'll probably have a few more "worst days ever" before the year is out. I'm telling you about this particular "worst day" not to bring you down, but to show you how you can rescue some good from even your bleakest day.

To begin with, the day was supposed to be super. I had gotten a call a couple of days earlier from the Fox News network. They wanted me to fly to New York to do a live interview in the studio that would be broadcast to some 30 million Americans. It would be an outstanding opportunity to sell myself and my first book, *Walk Like a Giant, Sell Like a Madman*. What could go wrong?

It started the night before. I had gone to bed around midnight and just could not get to sleep. The next morning I was tired and anxious. Then, the airline called to say my flight had been canceled. That meant that my wife, Kathy, had to drive me to a later flight, which upset our daughter, Kolleen, who could not get to the karate class she teaches. While I was on the way to the airport for my later flight, my office called to say one of my best and most experienced employees had quit that morning without giving any notice. This was a serious loss to my company and would have justified canceling my trip. I continued on because I was so committed to my overall plan, which included promoting my book.

It went on like that all day. At the airport, the only open seat on my new flight was in row 13. No, I'm not superstitious, but this did make me wonder a little bit. The airline had advertised free phone calls while in flight, which was great, but the phone system on the plane was not working, which was bad. I got into New York and the driver told me not to use my cell phone because of all the piracy going on.

Well, I finally got to the studio a few hours early. And they said, "Hello, Mr. Roberts, we're not quite ready for you yet but we'll let you wait in the greenroom," which of course is the waiting room for guests. I said, "Is there a phone in there?" And the producer said yes. I must have heaved this enormous sigh of relief. I finally was able to start making the calls I had needed to make all day.

The show itself turned out to be difficult, too. It was supposed to be an informational call-in show about real estate; but the other guest, who had never sold a home in her life, attacked everything I said. The producers were appalled.

Even so, by then I felt that my day had finally started to turn around. This is the point of this chapter. This is what I want you to remember. Things had gone so bad for me for the previous 12 hours that I just had to make something positive out of all this disappointment. That's my way to recover from a really bad day—I get moving again. I must have made 72 phone calls during the time before I went on the air—just one after the other. I called investors, customers, bankers. This is my way to pump myself up after a disappointment. It gets me past the immediate screw-ups and problems and gets back to a point where I'm working my plan.

By the time the Fox News people came for me to do the interview, I had regained some of my natural optimism and spirit. It didn't undo the loss of a key employee nor make up for my lack of sleep. But I did feel a whole lot more in control and on top of my game than I had an hour earlier. And just in time, too, because that was a pretty important interview.

RALPH'S RULE

Bad things happen to good salespeople all the time. But if you can channel that frustration and disappointment into positive energy, even your bad days will produce good results for you.

Are You Locked in a Box?

Everyone tells you to think "outside the box." Very few experts actually show you how it's done. We all know we're supposed to be creative. Yet most of the time we trap ourselves in the rut of looking at our problems in the same old way.

In this book I hope to cure you of that habit, because conventional thinking is not only unprofitable, it's downright dangerous for any salesperson who wants to still be in business in five or 10 years. Sales as a profession is changing faster than ever, and not always in ways that we like.

Take car sales. The automotive companies are drastically cutting back the number of dealerships as a way to streamline their marketing efforts—with the result that thousands of auto salespeople will be dismissed in the near future. Moreover, information available on the Internet allows millions of car buyers to shop from their homes or offices without ever talking to a salesperson.

Some car salespeople respond by just working longer hours, others by getting into another line of business. The more clever ones respond by creating their own Web pages, tapping into this important trend and capturing some of its magic for themselves.

Or consider my field, real estate. Probably one-third of all the Realtors now active will leave the profession within five years. Competition is getting too intense, and our customers, the ordinary American family trying to buy or sell a house, can find alternatives to brokers on the Internet or in a variety of other ways.

Again, there are routine ways to respond to this turning point in our business and there are extraordinary ways. Unfortunately, I'm convinced that most salespeople in any field respond to significant challenges first with denial—pretending the threat doesn't exist. And, second, most salespeople give up too early in the face of change, with the result that soon they're in another line of work, and blaming their bad luck or fate.

There are better ways to react to the challenges facing us all. Take me, for example. Reversals I've had during the past 23 years that I've sold real estate could have been enough to drive me from the business. Sky-high interest rates in the late 1970s, a time when I lost my own house to foreclosure, were just one of my many challenges. But through lean years and good years I've tried to see troubles as opportunities, not just as problems. I've tried to respond creatively, in nonroutine ways, in this never-ending campaign to grow my business. I'm convinced that in coming years I personally will be more successful than ever, no matter what trends trouble the profession at large.

To illustrate, I'm going to tell you about one of my more unorthodox efforts. It's my effort not only to see change coming but to harness it for my own good and that of my loved ones.

It's a fact that 25 percent of all the homes sold in America are sold by-owner—that is, without the services of a real estate sales-person like me. An owner simply posts a sign on the lawn, places a few newspaper ads, gets the word out by telling friends, and maybe posts a notice on the bulletin board at the grocery store. This trend is increasing. More info than ever is available on the Internet, empowering customers who don't like paying commissions to folks like us. From my own research, I estimate that in five years or so as many as 40 percent of all home transactions in the Detroit area, where I live and work, will be done by-owner. Where would you be in your field if 40 percent of your customers suddenly stopped using salespeople to get your product? Unless we salespeople adapt to this sort of trend, a lot of us will be out of business.

Now, most salespeople in my business react to this trend by telling for-sale-by-owner sellers how silly they are. Salespeople will call owners and try to convince them how badly they need the services of those salespeople. We've done that ourselves at Ralph R. Roberts Real Estate, Inc. But I also recognize that this approach can sometimes be a waste of effort. No doubt the seller already considered listing with an agent before deciding to go it alone. We don't change many minds simply by telling people they're dumb. Rather, we just annoy them.

So finally I hit on a way to tap into this trend of selling homes by-owner. I've created a concept to capture some of this business by selling people an entire kit to help them sell their homes themselves. It includes their lawn sign and business cards with the photo of their home printed on it and flyers listing all the important points about their house. But these kits include much more.

There's a training video to teach people the finer points of marketing their home. There's a 24-hour voice mail message service, so that by calling our messaging center and entering a five-digit code a prospective buyer can learn all about a home. We'll provide a pager to each customer until the transaction is complete. We're even considering offering the services of a home marketing specialist to help the customer understand how to handle this complex and important transaction.

As I write this, we're already formulating the plans to launch this effort in my suburban Detroit marketplace. Over the next couple of years, I hope to roll it out nationally.

I'm going on about this idea at length not to blow my own horn but to illustrate a point about creative thinking. This concept basically turns the assumptions of my profession upside-down. Some salespeople in my field—and even some in my own office—think I'm nuts for promoting the for-sale-by-owner idea. They think I'm helping to cut all our throats by showing customers how they don't need us. But I don't think so. As I said, probably at least one-fourth of all these sales will be done without us anyway. Why not dip into this enormous pool of business to come up with some revenue for ourselves?

Besides, a lot of homeowners fail to sell their homes by themselves, and eventually they do call a professional like me. If I've already established rapport with such customers, there's a good chance they'll call me if they can't sell their home themselves.

Why? Because I intend to run this new company as I do the rest of my business—with the customers' best interest in mind. You may think somebody like me—with 600 transactions a year to my credit—must cut corners and do some pretty slick deals. But I believe the opposite is true. I believe my success rests on a solid foundation of doing what's best for the customer year in and year out. Consider this: A huge amount of my business comes from repeat business and referrals—not the kind of business you get if you're tricking customers into using your services. You may do one deal that way, but you sure as heck won't be around in the long term, as I intend to be.

I see this as one of my most creative strokes. I'm convinced it'll be the next big thing in real estate sales. It won't replace my traditional home sales business; in fact, it probably will never amount to more than a small part of my overall business. But it's a great way to tap into a revenue stream that most salespeople have written off as lost. Besides, since I own mortgage, title, and building companies, I can generate more business by referring these for sale by-owner customers to those companies.

I was able to think up and then embrace this pretty radical idea because I'm not afraid of change or taking risks. And if there's one thing I want you to take away from this chapter and this book, it's this: Let's look at change as our friend, not our enemy.

RALPH'S RULE

Change can be scary, daunting, and uncomfortable. But within even the most threatening trend lies the spark of opportunity.

Final Thoughts

We just have time for a few more bits of wisdom gathered during 23 years on the front line of sales. If I had to distill everything I've learned, it would go like this:

Don't concentrate on making a lot of money. Concentrate on being the kind of person with whom other people want to do business.

Renew yourself at regular intervals with time off for family, friends, and hobbies.

God gave you two ears and one mouth. If you use them in that proportion, you'll come out right.

Embrace change, don't fear it. In every change lies the promise of new opportunity.

People have to know that you care before they care about what you know.

Don't settle for anything less than doing things just a little bit better than anybody else.

Take risks. It's better than piling up regrets.

Good planning remains the essence of time management.

A dishonest presentation is bad for your customer and will ruin your reputation.

Never badmouth the competition. It just cheapens you in the eyes of your customers.

Lunch hours are for talking to customers you can't reach during normal business hours.

Talent, education, and good looks may help, but not as much as hard work.

Remember the 80/20 rule. Eighty percent of your business comes from 20 percent of your clients.

Learn to delegate. If you don't have an assistant, you are one.

Maybe half your client base will change their jobs, their houses, or their financial circumstances within a year's time, so your marketing efforts have to be updated frequently.

Put your photograph on all your marketing materials. People can't buy from you if they don't know who you are.

Even after you're established, spend at least 5 percent of your budget on marketing and self-promotion.

Your most recent customer can be your hottest prospect for your next sale.

Most of my customers have bought or sold a home at least once before they met me. That means that some other salesperson didn't nurture that relationship enough to retain them.

Don't prejudge anybody. A waitress or a car valet may have a wider circle of acquaintances than anyone else you know.

Always remember to thank people. Thank them in person, thank them in writing, and don't forget to stay in touch.

A past customer or a referral should always take precedence over an entirely new customer.

If you don't ask, the answer is always no.

RALPH'S RULE

A book like this can help boost your productivity only if you put what you've learned into practice. Sell, sell, sell!

NOTE TO THE READER

Now that you've read *52 Weeks of Sales Success*, I'd like to invite you to be part of my next book. Please send me your own stories about salesmanship. I'd like to hear what works or doesn't work for you, who your heroes are, and what advice or techniques you've found especially helpful. You may e-mail your replies to me at ralphsworld@voyager.net, or send them via surface mail to Ralph R. Roberts Real Estate, Inc., 30521 Schoenherr, Warren, MI 48093. I sincerely hope to hear from you.

Thanks!
Best Wishes,

Ralph R. Roberts

INDEX